PATH OF FIRE

A Woman's Journey to Oneness

Elaine Heroux,LCSW

In memory of Tom: my love, my best friend and my rock

And to grandmothers everywhere

Let yourself be silently drawn
By the stronger pull
Of what you really love.

—Rumi

Contents

FOREWORD

In my work as an author, speaker, transpersonal facilitator and psychotherapist, I am aware that, just as an acorn bears within it the image and potential of a mighty oak tree, quite regardless of our birth or family or life experiences and regardless of the culture or other circumstances into which we are born, we are here to find and follow the plan and pattern of our Soul. In order to be happy and fulfilled, we must be true to that pattern.

I have known Elaine Heroux for thirty years. You will read here that in the very beginning of our transpersonal work together, she experienced a sudden illumination that tremendously augmented and accelerated her journey, opening her to a spiritual realm of which she, previously, was not consciously aware. Since that time I have more or less continuously known of most of the aspects of her voyage of discovery. Yet, though I already knew many of these details, on reading this manuscript I repeatedly have been struck with how fresh and alive and honest and captivating her story is. It clearly is written not from a mere ambition to be an author—to *impress*—but to express through her life story the vibrant message of the Soul. It also seems she had no choice but to write it, for the promptings of the Soul ultimately will not be denied.

Steve Jobs observed that life is like a game of 'connect the dots,' adding that, alas, the pattern reveals itself only in hindsight. Translating subconscious stipplings into a legible, visible tapestry often requires a lifetime of diligent work, made all the more challenging because it feels like groping in the dark to find one's way. Path of Fire lays out in everyday, relatable narratives the exquisitely meaningful life quest of this capable author.

Family, society, culture, and tradition—the outer trappings of civilization—all are devoted to comfort and safety and mediocrity. Some of its messages are "fit in," "be quiet," "don't rock the boat", "conform," "do as you are told," "don't make waves." But the Soul cries out for authenticity and creativity and living in attunement with our highest dreams. It calls us to live in ways that are superior to the ordinary, to dare to be a forerunner of a new and better way, even if that means being a misfit.

At a deep level, we know this when we are born but in the process of growing up most of us forget, losing touch with the essence of where we came from and what we are. A recent experience brought this sharply to my attention: my thirty-month-old granddaughter walked unannounced into the room and, with her palms upturned, asked, "What is this life about?" I was astonished that she would utter this deeply profound question at such a young age and responded, "What did you say, Molly?" She did not repeat it and I did not probe further, of course, but I had the distinct awareness that the question came not from her child's mind but from her Soul. English poet Rupert Brooke may have had a similar experience, prompting him to write "...there's wisdom of more than they have known, and thoughts go blowing through them are wiser than their own." Wiser, indeed!

Some of us seem destined to take up this ultimate search, as though haunted by invisible, subconscious promptings. Indeed the existential questions can haunt us, as Elaine Heroux experienced from early childhood. It is the good fortune of any reader of this book to accompany this author on her quest, chronicled through tales of life experiences that are always straightforward and yet so elegant in their simplicity.

Answering this question of 'what life is about' and finding our way back home often seems perilous. Usually we are surrounded by other people who also have lost their way. They advise and judge and cajole us, whether from concern for us or, perhaps more likely, fear that their own deeply buried questions might resurface.

"You'll never find what you're looking for," they may tell us. "Grow up!" "Stop daydreaming" they exhort. It is a lonely path, this journey back home—necessarily lonely, for it must be made alone. Most of us are consciously unaware of this, but at an unconscious level, we *know* that something is missing.

Do you know that inner longing? Most of us have it... and sometimes its call becomes so loud and persistent that plunging headlong into the dark unknown finally seems less frightening than continuing to ignore the relentless signals, as Elaine Heroux discovered. I believe this book will shed light in dark places for many people.

We can gauge the essence—the *truth*—of a thing by the feeling that lingers. I have experienced being with people who are purportedly advanced spiritually but noticing that I felt shut down or a bit dispirited afterward. Conversely, on other occasions I also have noticed that sometimes even a brief contact with an unpretentious, accepting person leaves me feeling uplifted and buoyant. I have come to recognize that the best indicator of the authenticity of a thing, then, is not thoughts but intuitive awareness and feelings. Such feelings and intuitive awareness, then, are the measure of essence.

So it is vital to pay attention to the 'field of consciousness.' As stated, we can discern the character of a thing by the vibration it engenders. When we read a book, we experience the energy of the author. This helps us to understand that it sometimes is difficult to keep our mind on a book written solely from a mental perspective, for it often is lacking in that divine aliveness of heart energy. This is one example of Jesus' teaching that 'by their fruits shall ye know them.' (Matthew 7:16 KJV) Stated differently, we can discern the essence of a thing by its vibration, by the level of consciousness it engenders.

The culture of the western world does not understand intuition and often disregards or suspects it. But the Soul sees around corners and silently conveys the true nature of a thing through its feeling tone. This, then, is the touchstone of authenticity.

Frankly, when I consented to write this Foreword, I was prepared to read the manuscript, even if tedious, and to say positive things. I was delighted from the first, however, to discover that I could hardly put the book down and I count it a blessing and a privilege to know this whole story. I feel honored to write this Foreword because I have read this book and know it to be full of love. When I finished reading the manuscript, the atmosphere in the room around me felt alive and filled with love—an experience of the unified field of consciousness.

The best spiritual books are written by those who are as though possessed by the spirit of the Divine. In this memoir, Elaine Heroux writes as one divinely possessed ... as an amanuensis of the Soul.

Dear Reader, a treat awaits you for Path of Fire emits a magnificent, ennobling vibration.

Christina Thomas-Fraser, M.A.
Encinitas, California
February 14, 2021

Books by Christina Thomas/Christina Thomas-Fraser

Secrets: A Practical Guide to Undreamed-of Possibilities
In Tune With The Soul
Change Your Patterns, Change Your Life

INTRODUCTION

I am now at the age at which I am considered an elder. Joseph Campbell, a renowned scholar and lover of mythology, wrote about the individual's search for purpose and meaning. He did this by using the metaphor of taking a trip through life from birth to old age and death.

Approaching our lives through the lens of travel and a quest for knowledge, allows us to make more sense of what we are experiencing on a day-to-day basis. This is how fiction writers plan a story. They ask themselves the questions: *Who is the hero? What are her/his challenges? How are those challenges resolved?*

Campbell outlined three main events of the journey: separation, initiation and returning home.[1] Returning home requires sharing with the community the treasure that was discovered so other people might benefit. I am at the last stage, and this is the story of my life with my healing guru, Haidakhan Babaji. It also relates my struggles to fully accept my knowledge and experiences of the Spirit World. It has been a process of finding the middle way of balance and creativity, and learning to trust my intuition and the world of dreams and of spirit. It is a journey with Babaji that went from longing and loneliness to meaning and purpose. I use these main steps of Campbell's theory to outline my own personal journey.

I offer my life experience as an example to others who may often feel lost, overwhelmed and confused by the vicissitudes of life, which may include challenges in relationships, finances, loss, poor health, disillusionment and too many more to mention. I, too, have frequently swum through, and almost drowned in, the energy and emotion required to cope with these problems, but I have realized that they are part of an overall picture of who we are and how we see ourselves and the world around us. They are part of the process of building self-knowledge and growing into the reality of our authentic selves. In each difficult and taxing experience is the potential for new life and a new way of seeing and being.

There really is a plan and a purpose for us, if only we take the time to listen and to take responsibility for ourselves. We are not doing this alone—we have Divine guidance and support along the way if only we acknowledge this and build a relationship with its source. We have a choice, and that is the beauty of it. What are you currently choosing in your life?

My hope is that some of the lessons I have learned along the way will benefit you as you negotiate the pitfalls, transcendence and mystery of this magnificent world.

I can recall Hurricane Dorian in 2019, as we waited to determine the direction and power of this force of nature as it hovered over the Bahamas. It reminded me of how Babaji came into my life over two decades ago. He entered my world like Dorian—suddenly, chaotically and with enormous power and unpredictability. The difference between the two is that today we have days to prepare for this epic hurricane force. We are told how big it is, how quickly it is moving, what to expect and how to prepare. Two decades ago, I had no way of knowing that Babaji was hovering on the horizon. There was no team of experts to inform me of His possible impact.

Babaji is a Mahavatar, which means He was not born of a woman. This is significant, because in the Hindu scriptures the term signifies the descent of Divinity into flesh. It is a sign of the total embodiment of the Divine in human form. Spiritually advanced to the point where He can materialize and de-materialize at will, Babaji was discovered as a young man, meditating in a cave in the Himalayas, in 1970. It is said by Babaji's devotees that He was the reincarnation of Lahiri Mahasaya's guru, who was written about by Paramahansa Yogananda in *Autobiography of a Yogi*.[2] The 1970 Babaji was in his body for only 14 years before he passed into the next world on Valentine's day in 1984.

Babaji entered my life in 1991, which was almost a decade after He left this earth. "How did He do that?" you may ask. I will tell you.

My desire is to give hope to all people who are struggling with themselves and life in general, and wondering about the meaning of it all. A gifted artist (writer, visual artist, sculptor and more) understands that she will never know what her completed project will look like. She just trusts the creative process and knows that a beautiful work of art, even a masterpiece, will emerge at the end of it. This is a metaphor for life and how we live it. We are the artists and co-creators of our own lives. In the same way the artist uses tools and colors and words to assist her with her creative pursuit, we have certain utensils available to us as we move through our lives. These are aids that assist us on our inner journey—providing enormous understanding, comfort and strength. I am sharing with you the gifts that I discovered in my life in the hope that you can start searching for yours.

I say I was unprepared for Babaji's arrival, and yet, when I look back, it's as if all the years leading to that fateful encounter were a preparation of sorts, although I would never have known it at the time. He was to initiate huge energetic shifts in my physical, emotional and spiritual worlds. He demolished my life the way it was and rebuilt it with a structure of love and stability. He did this by helping me work on my inner world of beliefs, conscious thoughts and feelings. He initiated an inner journey where He was, and still is, my constant guide and companion.

Robert Johnson, in his book *Balancing Heaven and Earth*[3] talks about slender threads that give meaning to us and create the tapestry of our lives. These are moments of synchronicity or fate that remind us of a power at work that is greater than ourselves. I like to call them *silver threads* and to see them as points where the Divine meets the normality or mundaneness of everyday living. I was so captured by this idea that I had a burning desire to finally verbally lay out my own tapestry as I attempted to gain clarity and share it with others. I found that in looking back through seven decades of living, it was so much easier to take a different perspective on one's life. Like widening the lens in a microscope, we can see with more clarity the context, rather than the content, of our experiences when our vantage point is from our later years.

As I have written about the second half of my life, I have realized that my relationship with Babaji has been a part of myself that I have split off and never fully owned. In the Babaji community, I could relax a little more, as I felt more understood by my spiritual family. It seemed that all of us were unique and very different from each other, yet we mostly practiced tolerance and acceptance, and we had faith in each other that we were coming from the same spiritual teachings. It is very sad to me that few people talk about the inner world, and fewer recognize the huge divide between it and community life. How are we expected to cross this divide if we are not able to talk about it?

I grew up in a very conservative, simple home where children were expected to be seen and not heard, and raised with strict English norms of appropriate and polite behavior. It took just a few instances of being my authentic self as a child to realize it was not acceptable to others who failed to understand me. Therefore, the outside world represented a threat to me as I grew older. My greatest fear was to be considered weird or strange, so I protected all my beliefs that did not fit with the collective ideas. The problem with this approach was that the box I had put myself into was becoming smaller and smaller, and increasingly more uncomfortable, as I became its prisoner. I realized I was keeping secrets and using up a great deal of energy in doing so. Any secret is based on shame, so keeping a secret from other people meant that I was keeping it from myself.

My life outside the Babaji community has been one of conformity and practicality. No one would ever have known my innermost feelings and beliefs. This is one reason for wanting to share my journey with a wider audience.

A second reason for writing *Path of Fire* is that we are now living in very divisive and angry times. The recent 2020 election has revealed the extent of the split in the United States, where each half of the population has a completely different desire for the direction of the country moving forward. My spiritual path has taught me that there are no simple answers, that it's important to have understanding and compassion even as we are willing and courageous enough to stand up to evil and bad intentions.

In 2020, we also faced the world pandemic of COVID-19, which has killed millions and required people to quarantine themselves in their homes in order to avoid spreading this virus even further. We are bombarded by opinions and judgments on all sides as we all try to understand the best and safest way to move forward. In our country and the world in general, we are facing an international dark period.

Throughout this all, my guru is my rock and my polestar. I often wonder where I would be without this level of security in my life, with chaos all around me.

I want you to understand that you can take a different road which will lead you off the beaten track that is trodden by most people in our times. This path is also vastly different from the one we are encouraged to take by the collective and most of the people around us. It is an emotional and spiritual inner journey, and one that leads us to the soul of who we are. It is my belief that we can never achieve peace in a country or in the world until more people have made this inner journey to their own soul. At this time especially, we are being called to walk this inner path and stand strong in our values and our faith.

Thus, I am sharing this healing journey with all those who are open and will listen. It has taken me more than 70 years to get to where I am today, and increasingly, I believe that we no longer have the leisure of time. It seems imperative that we develop spiritually as quickly as possible, so we become beacons of light to all those who are still blindly stumbling around in the darkness. More than ever, we also need strong communities of like-minded people who can hold the fabric of our world together when it seems to be collapsing around us. Unknowingly, many have been preparing for these times and are functioning as stars of light in the universe. They are here, creating a web of Divine support that can contain the chaotic energy, educate others, and provide hope for the future.

The mortal/human world is not our real home, so how do we create a life that honors our humanity and at the same time, explores, understands and accepts the spiritual world? We need a trustworthy Guide who can help us do this and who provides unconditional love and support. Babaji has been that guide for me and is available for anyone who is willing to be guided.

It's important to note that there are hundreds of thousands of different teachers available to us. How do we know if they can be trusted? In retrospect, there were times when I put my trust in those who seemed to be the wrong people. Were they really the "wrong" people, though? For in each instance, I learned more, and they brought me closer to self-understanding. These people unwittingly taught me how to trust myself.

What I ultimately discovered was that good teachers are unwavering in their teachings yet are not interested in power and control over us. They will share their wisdom and teachings if we ask. They are imbued with respect, and their love for self and others is palpable. They do not believe they have all the answers for themselves or anyone else, and they recognize that we all have our unique path to oneness.

Sadly, it is all too easy to project the best parts of ourselves onto teachers and guides and to feel "less than" because of it. A good teacher will recognize this and refuse to accept the projection by encouraging their students to look inward. A therapist can help us understand these projections and blind spots that we are carrying.

It helps enormously if we have a psychological understanding of ourselves. In my profession as a psychotherapist, I am daily reminded of the importance of having insight into our psychological makeup. Why do we make certain destructive decisions repeatedly? Why do we attract the same kinds of people and situations into our lives that cause enormous pain and hardship? This has nothing to do with our spiritual beliefs but almost always is the result of faulty ideas that develop in our formative years. Once we understand this, we can use our spiritual wisdom to help us overcome these beliefs. However, we must do the work to transform psychological and emotional problems into the gifts that come from healing. I would call this the spiritual work.

As I spend my time semi-quarantined in Florida and surrounded by chaos, I remember the words of one of my teachers, Marion Woodman, who said, "There is no birth without a death or a rebirth."[4] I think of this often during these difficult times. My sense and hope are that, collectively, we are birthing a new way of being—and this is the beginning of the death of what was.

The story you're about to read is my own personal account of being born into a new existence. It is a journey that took me from my earliest years to understanding the impact of those times. It is a slow process that moved me from my head into my heart, from spirit to soul and from the masculine to the feminine. It just makes sense that if we can be transformed individually, we can also be transformed as a culture, a country and ultimately as a species. We cannot consciously alter the larger picture, but we can definitely begin to take responsibility for changing ourselves. By doing that, we can ultimately change the world. This gives us enormous hope for the future. In the words of Lao Tzu, "A journey of a thousand miles begins with a single step." I invite you to take that step today.

Notes

[1] Joseph Campbell, *The Hero's Journey.*

[2] Paramahansa Yogananda, *Autobiography of a Yogi*, pp. 296-304.

[3] Robert Johnson. *Balancing Heaven and Earth*, Prologue xi

[4] Marion Woodman. *Marion Woodman Foundation BodySoul Rhythms®️ Leadership Training Workshops.*

PART 1

THE MOLD INTO WHICH WE ARE BORN

Most people do not feed their souls because they do not know how. Most of us in this culture are brought up by parents who like the rest of society are running as fast as they can, trying to keep up financially, socially and every other way. . . . Often the parent isn't able to receive the soul of the child, whatever the little soul is, because the parent doesn't take time to receive or doesn't like what the child is. . . . Children who are not loved in their very beingness do not know how to love themselves. As adults, they have to learn to nourish, to mother their own lost child.[1]

—*Conscious Femininity*,
by Marion Woodman: Inner City Books

1.
BEGINNINGS

Once upon a time, a baby girl was born in the United Kingdom to a young couple who welcomed her with open arms. They nicknamed her Toot or Toots, since she was a fussy baby and often crying.

Her father said, "There she is, tooting again," and the name stuck. She came into the world during a time of jubilation, rebuilding and scarcity. England was in the process of recovery from the Second World War. While there was celebration for the end of the war, there was also a challenging transition to a more peaceful era, as damaged towns and war-torn London, as well as a suffering economy, had to be rebuilt.

Not remembering this personally, Toots learned about it later from reading and talking to friends and family members. The war had also taken its emotional toll, as young men who survived returned home and would hardly be recognized by their loved ones because of the trauma of what they had lived through. There were also thousands of people to whom their husbands and sons would never return, and the grief of that could never be expunged.

The war was a shadow or enigma for Toots as she heard about these men and noticed the reclusive behavior of those who had returned. She heard family members whispering, "It was the war, you know—he came home a different man."

She found ration books hidden away in an old wooden chest and asked her mother what they were. Her mother explained that when she was pregnant with Toots, she stood in line for an apple at the local grocery store with her ration coupons. By the time the queue wound down and she was second in line, she was told that the store had just sold its last apple. Hearing the news, she broke down into racking sobs, which resulted in her being given an apple by a generous customer who was just leaving. Another war reminder for Toots was the Sunday radio program called Forces Favorites, which she listened to with regular and great enjoyment as she grew older. The war years became more real to her as Vera Lynn belted out patriotic songs in her beautiful, unique, strong voice.

Toots' father was a mechanical engineer who was forced to leave school when he was 17, with no hope of continuing his education. His father, a carpenter, was hit by an oil bomb at the beginning of the war and was treated for extensive burns, which prevented him from working for many months. Being the eldest child, Toots' father inherited the breadwinner position in the family, requiring that he work full time and take money home to feed a family of five. This had an enormous impact on him, as he was maturing into a young man and he never quite recovered from the responsibility. He spent the rest of his life guarding his money as closely as a jailer would guard his prisoner.

Toots' mother was another story, since fate had handed her a different challenge that haunted her until the day she died. She was raised in an orphanage in South Wales. In 1925, when she was two years old, her father divorced her mother, leaving her with three young children. Toots' mum was the youngest child. In those times, it was unheard of for women to be alone raising a family, and the only employment that was *available to her mother's mother was in domestic service. (You may be familiar with the hiring of live-in maids by upper-class families through the PBS series* Upstairs, Downstairs, *and later,* Downton Abbey.*) Toots' maternal grandmother was accepted into service but was only allowed to take one of her children with her. Sadly, she was forced to make this impossible decision and chose to keep the eldest daughter, while the younger ones were sent to an orphanage. It was at the orphanage that Toots' mum was to live for the next 14 years.*

When Toots' mum was 16 years old, her father suddenly appeared to take her home. She was now old enough to work, and he saw her as another wage earner. She was taken away from the only home she could remember and moved into his house to live with him and his new wife. Both were strangers to her. The atmosphere in this house was cold and distant, and she rarely talked about it in her later years. She found war work sewing parachutes at a garment factory, and her only enjoyment was spending time with her friends at the local dance hall. She met Toots' dad at one of these dances, and he became a fierce protector and helped her move into "digs" (shared accommodation) where she would be with other girls and become more independent.

Toots' parents were married when her dad was 21 and her mum was 19. Toots came along two years later. Of course, she knew none of these things when she came into the world on a blustery, cold November day. She was to learn about them piece by piece, like grains of sand that are slowly piled one on the other until they morph into a larger form in a complex sand structure.

Being an only child, she was pampered and spoiled in the first few years of her life. Her memories included that of her father painting huge Mickey Mouse murals on her bedroom wall and riding his bike into town one Christmas to buy her a prized rocking horse that came home with him on the bike. There were also large birthday parties that were enjoyed by everyone except Toots herself. All the neighborhood kids would be invited for cake and sandwiches, and to watch a film that was shown on an old-fashioned projector, while Toots, an introvert from an early age, would fold into herself like a Murphy bed.

Toots adored her father. He was the kindest of souls, and almost all the caring and understanding that she received, came from him. Given her mother's tragic and lonely upbringing, she just did not have any affection to give. Toots' mothering came from her father, who doted on her as tenderly as he nurtured the roses in his garden, for which he won many prizes. He was a gentle man of few words who avoided conflict. Toots placed her father on a pedestal for many years of her life.

In contrast, her relationship with her mother was very volatile and complex. There was a festering wound in her mum that never healed due to her early abandonment. Because of this trauma, her emotional growth became arrested, and she was a two-year-old in a mother's body. Today, she may have been diagnosed with a bipolar disorder. She was depressed, but her friends would never have known this.

As she grew older, Toots often felt unhinged by her mother and her moods. Her mum was always the life and soul of the party and could sometimes be really funny. Her friends adored her, and they would ask Toots questions like, "What did you do to deserve a mother like her?" These words were said with such admiration and would cause enormous confusion for Toots, who thought, Why do I not see her this way? Why is she so different at home?

She began to believe that she was somehow causing her mum to be so moody. Sometimes, Toots felt sad and invisible. When she was noticed, she was always doing things wrong and making her mum angry. She was frustrated because she didn't know how to make her mum happy, and she felt like a cork being tossed around on a stormy sea.

The first seismic fault in the home landscape appeared around the time Toots started school at age five. At that time, her mother became pregnant again and was preparing her daughter for a baby brother. One day, her mother suddenly disappeared, and Toots learned that she was in the hospital. Nobody ever told her why she had been taken there. and she was just left to figure things out for herself when her mum returned home alone. The baby brother was never mentioned again. Asking no questions and "figuring things out" were to set a precedent for Toots for most of her life.

Toots became different after that incident, which became written indelibly on her heart. Her mother was now cocooned in a fog of despair. Toots didn't know that's what it was—she just understood that the mum she knew was no longer there. Trying to talk to her was like dropping a pebble in her great grandmother's very deep well and never hearing it hit the water. It felt very dark, as a thick blanket descended over the entire house. It was then that she began to carry the grief and anger that were locked so deeply inside her mother. It was as if she grew into an adult child overnight, and from that time forward, at least until she entered analysis as an adult, she felt responsible for the life and feelings of a mother who was emotionally wounded.

Not long after this, Toots' maternal grandmother resurfaced in her mum's life after years of absence. There were a few letters that appeared with increasingly greater insistence until her mother finally acknowledged them. Toots overheard *conversations explaining that her grandmother wanted to now meet the daughter she had dropped off at the orphanage when she was two years old.*

Toots was never directly told about this until one day she was bundled up in the car and her dad drove them to a house where she was entertained by a young girl while her mother and grandmother reunited. Toots remembered her mother saying on the way home, "I only went to meet her out of curiosity, and I felt absolutely nothing for her—nothing." She then went on to pronounce, "I will never have anything to do with that woman again."

No feelings toward her ? Hmm...*thought Toots. As young as she was, she knew how angry her mum felt toward this stranger who had returned to claim her after a 30-year absence.*

Toots' feelings of being responsible for her mother would intensify and be firmly entrenched when her father was promoted to Overseas Engineer about three years later and would start traveling with his company. The anger and grief metastasized like a cancer as mother and daughter were left alone for four months at a time. Periodically, the anger would erupt from one or the other of them. There would be shouting and histrionics, interspersed with complete silence.

For Toots, it was a time of waiting—waiting for her dad to return so they could go back to some semblance of normalcy. The problem was, there was a new normal being established. Father would return home, and within a week or two, he would choose to leave rather than discuss the anger and frustration they were living with. If he stayed longer, Toots began to resent the disruption in their usual routine, as he automatically took ownership of the decision-maker role. She resented this, since she knew they had been perfectly capable of making their own decisions while he was away.

Toots felt guilty and confused by these feelings and began to see that Father's halo was somewhat tarnished. This was because she kept asking herself: Why is he unable to communicate his true feelings? Why does he choose to stay away for months on end, leaving us to fend for ourselves? Why does he feel he has the right to tell us what to do and change the rules of our home?

She would ask him why he couldn't find different work where he could be home all the time, and she would always get the answer, "This job allows you to have a better life than you would have otherwise." This was another confusing idea for a young child who thought that a family together would be the better life.

This was an indication to Toots of the importance her dad placed on the material world and the power created by one's earning potential. At one point when she was a teenager, he told her, "You are only as good as your earning power." This was a powerful sentence that her body immediately rejected. She had conflict with it for a great many years, as she suffered from a poverty consciousness believing that money was intrinsically bad. She strived to prove that money was insignificant and that her value was more than just how much she could earn. Over time, she came to terms with the fact that money is only energy and is neither good nor bad. It was, however, necessary to put a roof over one's head and food on the table.

During that time when her father was traveling, she was caught in a fantasy world that was dotted with moments of reality. When the confusion, overwhelm and loneliness became too intense, she would retreat to her inner world, where she felt safe and secure. This, too, set a precedent for her future, as she struggled to stay grounded between the spiritual world and the mundane, often painful, human existence.

Life started to improve when she went to high school. Her new friends became a healing salve to her tortured soul during her teenage years. She borrowed their sense of fun and adventure. She learned to love books. Their families became her adopted families, and she could not wait to spend weekends with them and experience the kind of home life she never had. She spent weekends lolling in the haystacks at one friend's farm and went to another friend so they could escape to the Mecca Ballroom on Saturday nights to dance and be entertained by the great Tom Jones. She and a third friend fell in love with horses and would go riding every week, as well as hold gymkhanas in the back garden with horses made from broomsticks with stuffed sock heads.

It was a carefree time. She discovered herself with her friends, and it was a Self that she liked better than the one who found herself in constant combat with her mother and in confusion and idealization around her father. She began to test her wings, and she liked the feeling of a growing freedom.

There were other ways she learned to cope with this lonely and unstable life. Throughout all these years, her paternal grandmother became her confidant and anchor. She helped keep Toots sane and grounded. She loved Toots with her home-cooked food and fireside conversations. Nan was one of 11 children who were born into humble beginnings. Her mother never worked as far as Toots knew, and her father was a gravedigger and a groundskeeper on a local estate. He was a man of the earth. Nan went into service when she was 16 years old and met Toots' granddad during this time. Nan was always kind and loving to Toots and would talk to her like an equal. She had a simple, practical view of the world and was wonderfully comfortable to be with. Toots never felt that she had to act a certain way with her. She could be herself, and Nan understood who that was.

Nan was one of two constants in Toots' life. The other constant was the Divine Mother in the form of Mother Earth. She offered Toots peace and tranquility, although at that age she had no direct knowledge of Her. Toots' favorite pastime was to go fishing in the local stream, which was within walking distance of her home. At that time, in a small town in England it was safe to wander a few hundred yards from home (and even a mile or two to get into town) and congregate with other kids or spend precious alone time in the local field. Getting to the stream required crossing a cow pasture, rich in green grass and yellow buttercups and dotted with cow pancakes that had to be carefully negotiated. The stream was a gently flowing, narrow body of water that was accessible to an eight-year-old in some hidden spots that few knew about. Sliding down the bank on her behind and wearing her trusted wellies (Wellington boots), Toots was able to get into the brackish water and wade almost knee deep as she thrust her fishing net under the weeds that were growing from the sides of the bank. Pulling the net out was always an exciting moment of anticipation as she peered closely to discover the treasures she had captured.

The baby minnows were her favorite, and they immediately went into a jam jar filled with water and brought along especially for this purpose. Toots always returned home very satisfied with her expedition and usually carried with her some frog spawn along with the minnows. This always caused problems for her mother, as the spawn hatched into tadpoles and finally became frogs. Occasionally, she would go to the stream with a friend so they could each take two corners of a large handkerchief that would catch a larger hoist of treasures.

Moments like these forged in Toots a deep and abiding love and respect for nature. She took for granted the fact that she felt intrinsically connected to the natural world around her. Being outside was nourishment for her soul and provided a feeling of contentment and deep fulfillment that would enable all her childhood worries to fade away. She would walk around the country lanes close to her friend's farm. She learned to love the subtle contours of the hills and the wildflowers and berries peering out of their homes in dense hedgerows. In this, she sensed the continuity of life. As a baby recognizes and blends in with her mother's body when she cuddles into her lap, so she remembered the curves of Mother Earth in this village, and the effect they had on her.

Another memorable incident with Mother Nature came when Toots visited her great grandmother's home. A widow, she lived in a small cottage in the middle of a heath in Norfolk. The heath was home to hundreds of rabbits before most of them were wiped out by a Myxomatosis disease in the 1950's. This is a highly contagious viral disease that was discovered in 1953 and fatal to European rabbits. As they drove down the long, rutted path toward the cottage, hundreds of white tails bobbed as they were dispersed to the safety of their burrows. Along the front of the cottage ran a low boxwood hedge from which emanated the most evocative perfume. Toots would inhale huge gulps of this scent, which she felt was welcoming and beckoning her inside. It was a smell that she learned to associate with her great grandmother.

There was no electricity in the cottage and no running water. It didn't matter—Toots dined on feasts of cooked rabbit and pheasant that were prepared on a steel plate over a continuously burning fire. The back of the cottage revealed a well for her water, and beyond that, the edges of a forest.

On one particular visit, she had gone out into the forest and was attracted to a chestnut tree. It called to her because of its low branches—a cool, sheltering umbrella. Having found a way to climb its branches, she spent the entire afternoon sitting in the tree eating chestnuts. It felt like her own secret hideaway, where she could watch the animal world go by and was invisible to all people. Finally, after a few hours, she reluctantly climbed down and returned to the cottage with a stomach full of chestnuts and a heart full of happiness.

You may have realized by now that this is the story of my early life. I use the word *story* because we all have a story to tell about our childhoods. These stories may not always be absolutely true, but that does not matter. The messages we have learned to believe about ourselves, however, do matter. They will inform the rest of our lives until we become conscious of them. We carry these beliefs into adulthood until we realize that they are not working for us, and in most cases, not even true.

I tell my story because it provides the backdrop to the family into which I was born. Call it fate, karma, good luck or plain bad luck—our parents and ancestors contribute significantly to how we see ourselves and the beliefs that we adopt or create in our formative years. Whether we like it or not, we are a product of our genes, and we can learn a great deal about ourselves and our beliefs by knowing and understanding more about the lives of our parents and grandparents. We carry the emotions and the culture of our heritage in our blood and the cells of our bodies.

None of this is being told to denigrate my parents at all, or indeed, any parents. I am relating it to explain my perception of my early years and how my own personal myth came into being. I now know they were the best parents they knew how to be, especially considering that they were saddled with enormous challenges in their own lives. How they parented was influenced by the time in which they lived, as well as the limitations that were handed down by their parents before them. I have heard it said that the sins of the father are handed down for seven generations. This does not refer to sins in a literal sense, but more to values, beliefs and ways of coping in the world. The latter are all lived out in an unconscious manner until we become aware of them.

Recently, I began to wonder about their side of the story. I think they would both say they did their best to be good parents. My mum would be upset that I was revealing family secrets and/or telling untruths about her. She would also say I was a difficult child, and indeed, I may have been. My dad, I think, would be shocked that I would suggest he was not a good husband and provider. It was important for him to be seen that way. He dedicated his life to his work and his family, and his wife and daughter were his reason for working as hard as he did. He had been taught to do so, and his life experience had taught him that people economically depended on him. He would have believed he was generous and gave us both a good life. This was all true, and he was successful according to the mores of the time in which he lived. These were the expectations of his community and family, and he more than lived up to them.

I came along in a different generation. It was the end of the war, and we were entering the Age of Aquarius, which was to herald the revelation of truth and the expansion of consciousness. We were standing on the cusp of a new era of independence for women, and the birth control pill was to become a legal form of contraception in the United States in 1960. Women were slowly being liberated from the shackles of their ancestors and were beginning to enjoy a newfound freedom. I would be growing up in a completely foreign world than the one my parents were used to.

Having said that, sometimes as adults with a desire to be loyal to our parents, it is all too easy for us to rationalize away our early memories and never fully embrace our truths. Our personal story is unique to us and must be fully inhabited before we can move to understand our parents. We have to accomplish the hard work of connecting to and releasing all the feelings surrounding our story before we can forgive, understand and move forward. There is no skipping a step and no easy way to negotiate this, and it can often be brutal. This is a healing process on which many of us are called to embark.

As part of my healing, I had to understand my mother and where she came from. She turned out to be instrumental in my search for Babaji. This search was initially unconscious, but it was always inside me from the beginning. Who can imagine the depth of pain my mother endured, knowing that her mother could part with her own baby? If she was unlovable as a baby, when would she ever be lovable? That was the belief she took from this ultimate abandonment. This belief played out in our relationship and has contributed to my thinking I was unlovable for most of my life. No matter how hard we tried to love each other, it was always clumsy and like a strange dance where we were both out of step.

When she met my dad, she was missing the orphanage and all the children. Mum used to tell tales of her life in the orphanage. She talked about it in glowing terms and conveniently glossed over the fact that she had been abandoned by her father and mother at a tender age. She fondly remembered Lady, who ran the orphanage, and would reminisce about her often. Mum recounted tales of being Lady's favorite child and talked about what she did to curry favor with her. She painted a perfect picture where real feelings are hidden away in dark colors on the canvas that was her life. Occasionally, I would see glimpses of the devastation as she talked about visitors' day every month. She would dress in her best clothes and wait patiently, hoping with fervor that her mother or father would visit. If not them, dare she hope that maybe another visitor would arrive solely to visit her? No one ever came, so she would pack away her clothes and go through the same hope and disappointment the following month. This was to go on until her father finally showed up when she was 16. For the second time in 16 years, she would be torn away from yet another mother figure to whom she had been attached.

I often thought that Dad was deeply affected by Mum's early life, which caused him to rescue her from the unhappy situation with her father. I imagine it appealed to his Sir Galahad fantasy of being a knight in shining armor and his desire to carry her away to a life of love, happiness, safety and security. He definitely succeeded in the latter goals, but unknown to him at the time, he was never able to help her overcome the extraordinary trauma she had survived. Nothing would make her happy, nor would anyone be able to truly love her in a healthy way.

After she had the miscarriage, Mum was never the same after she came home, having left a large part of her soul at the hospital with the baby. I remember the confusion and sadness that took up its dark residence in the house. It was never acknowledged or talked about, but was felt acutely by me. I know now that she experienced enormous trauma with the loss of this child. It is well known that the soul goes into hiding when it cannot handle the stress of the situation it finds itself in. We see this all the time in our veterans who come home with post-traumatic stress disorder (PTSD). Ed Tick, in his book *War and the Soul*, acknowledges this when he describes

PTSD as a deep wounding to the soul, which is one of the most horrific results of combat.

It is significant that I would have such a memorable feeling sense of this situation, in that it reveals my heightened sensitivity to the energy around me. This was with me from an early age and became one of my handicaps, as well as one of my greatest gifts. It was a handicap in that I grew up taking in the feelings of others and believing they were mine, and my greatest gift in that it provided me with empathy and understanding of the people around me. In today's words, I would be considered an empath, and many people find themselves in therapy because of these qualities. Also, it seems that the emotional boundaries between mother and daughter are frequently blurred and porous. It is easy to carry pain for each other, never knowing where the personal pain begins and the pain of the other ends. This may have something to do with the fact that we were born from our mother's body and have an intimate womb experience of her and the emotions she lived with.

Even as I write this now, I feel enormous sadness for my mother, as well as sadness for myself. It was a tough road for both of us, yet I am clear that this provided me with the impetus to ultimately leave my family, as I was drawn by an umbilical cord to something far greater than I could predict or imagine.

Notes

[1] Marion Woodman, *Conscious Femininity*, p. 45.

However we define "soul", we know it when we encounter it. We don't have to ask. We are suffused with it.[1]

—*Coming Home to Myself*
by Marion Woodman and Jill Mellick: Conari Press

2.
EARLY GLIMPSES OF SOUL

What was your favorite book or movie as a child? Did you have recurring dreams? The answers to these questions can tell you a great deal about your young, impressionable soul. What role did you play in your family? Were you the caregiver, the scapegoat, the comedian, the peacemaker, the teacher, the athlete? The answers to these questions can inform your life.

We are born with a soul that is immortal and an intrinsic part of who we are as a unique individual. It is the part of us that communicates with spirit and resonates with everything that is good and beautiful. It reveals itself in poetry, music and the arts. It carries our values and inspiration and our will to create. It produces our imagination and the ability to love deeply. It frequently is beyond words and reveals itself in images. As children, we are often more connected to our souls than we may be as adults because we are closer to a non-verbal 'knowing' about things. We resonate with certain characters or stories without questioning or really knowing why.

One of the core components of Carl Jung's theory of psychology is the notion of archetypes. These are universal patterns that live in the collective unconscious and form the foundation for movies, fairy tales and mythology. We recognize them in the themes we see daily in popular culture. Since they live in the unconscious, we can align ourselves unknowingly with a certain archetype and live it out in our lives. For example, we can live out the archetype of the hero, the mother, the warrior etc.

The most prominent archetype that I aligned with in my life was that of the Orphan. The motif behind this archetype is that of the abandoned child.

I clearly remember as a child that my favorite movie was called *Pollyanna*. The film came out in 1960 and starred Hayley Mills, the young daughter of the then famous actor Sir John Mills. It tells the story of a young teen who is orphaned suddenly when her missionary parents die. She goes to live with her elderly spinster aunt in a small town where the aunt has some prominence. The movie reveals the young girl's indominable spirit as she refuses to be intimidated by her somewhat abusive aunt and sets out to befriend everyone in the town. The term *Pollyanna* originates from the book that birthed this movie and is used to refer to people who have an optimistic approach to life.

Hayley Mills and I were about the same age, and at 14 years old, I related to her character in the movie. I remember the tears streaming down my face as I drank in every word and feeling that came off the movie screen. I readily identified with this young girl and felt her pain of loneliness and loss. There was no one who really cared for her (her aunt took her in because of a social obligation), and although she was alone in the world, she made the best of it and people responded favorably to her. There was an unspoken lesson for me that I could do the same, and this gave me hope. It had enormous impact on me moving forward.

What is it like to have an orphan character? I have memories of always feeling like an outsider, as if there was a joke everyone was sharing and I had been left out of the loop. When I tried to be myself, the responses were always different but nobody ever seemed to really listen and hear me. Some people took a step away from me and looked at me in shock, others told me I was too sensitive and my mother would deny the truth of what I was trying to convey. I quickly learned that my kind of truth was not shared by many people. I became secretive and introverted, and I played along with others even if I never totally agreed with them. My truth became hidden and fiercely protected. It was a lonely life.

One result of this orphan psychology is that I never felt I fit in. Other kids had brothers and sisters and a mother and father in the home. (This was during the time couples generally stayed together regardless of how they felt about each other.) My friends' mothers were nurturing and around all the time, while mine worked part time and was preoccupied when she was physically present.

I was acutely aware of the instances and times that I felt "different" from the people around me. An example comes to mind that epitomizes this.

When I was quite young, I knew of a boy who collected his pocket money all year in order to buy his mother a special Christmas gift. A few days before Christmas, he set off by himself, walking to town with great excitement. He scoured the shops and finally found the perfect gift. It was a beautiful Christmas tree ornament—large and round and covered with silver and gold sequins. He had just enough money to buy it, and the shopkeeper wrapped it gently in tissue paper before the boy very carefully placed it in the pocket of his jacket. It was with some jubilation and a newly found feeling of independence that he set off for home with his treasure in his pocket. He arrived home to find that all the doors to the house were locked. He walked all around the house, and then to the front door, and rang the doorbell. It was then, while waiting for his mother to answer and harboring great relief that he was almost home, he leaned against the side of the house and smashed the ornament into a million pieces.

This is a true story, and I remember very clearly how his mother laughed about it as she recounted the tale. I felt very sad for the boy, and although I was only about ten years old, I intuitively sensed this was telling me something particularly important about life. It was to be many more years before I understood the significance for me. I knew the boy had gone to great lengths to find a treasure for his mother that was destroyed. At some level, I was in touch with the archetypal world from a very young age. Had the boy known about the power of the myth, he would have known how important it was to safeguard the treasure he brought home from his mini hero's journey.

Myths are sacred stories that tell of man's experience in the world around him. They are sacred because they recount relevant stories about life and overcoming its challenges. They frequently feature heroes facing and overcoming adversity. They provide hope and guidance for our life's journey. People can relate to mythical characters and the lessons that are laid down in the stories.

There are such a variety of myths and fables around that it is not difficult to find tales that are relevant to our own life. There are stories of the masculine experience and stories of the feminine, and our interest does not have to be aligned with our own gender. We all carry both masculine and feminine qualities, whether we are in a male or female body.

I mentioned before that I was drawn to Campbell's hero's journey, which is focused mainly on the male experience. Somehow, the stages resonated with me. At some point, I also read a book that related the hero's journey from a woman's perspective. At the time I read it, it did not speak to me in the same way. Now I know I was entrenched in the masculine world and understood it better. I was to learn about my wounded feminine much later, after Babaji came into my life. This indicates that so much of our learning is about timing. We find the right teachers and learn the necessary lessons in the right time. When I look back, I can see this reflected in my experiences over and over again.

I see the last stage of Campbell's hero's journey of bringing home the treasure and sharing it with the community as a gift of soul and lessons that can be handed down from one generation to another. The treasure is the culmination of wisdom and understanding that we have built through the years into the seasoned soul of who we are. I know now that the reason I felt so sad was because the boy had undertaken a very loving and serious quest, and he'd inadvertently destroyed the treasure as he approached the end of his quest. That is like living into old age and not realizing we are carrying gold that we can share, or worse still, not realizing our life has had any value.

Back then, I was confused because everyone was laughing about this poor boy. Obviously, something was wrong with me that I felt so sad for him. I now realize that the sadness for him was because his mother did not understand this soul gift that had been shattered in a moment of thoughtlessness, and she had responded with humor.

As I write this, I realize that, for as long as I can remember, I believed that my life was a journey and that I really did not fit into this family and strange world I found myself in. In mid-life, I resonated with Clarissa Pinkola Estes' book, *Women Who Run with the Wolves*. I loved her storytelling and the lessons I heard behind the tales. She painted pictures of freedom, uniqueness and independence that I did not feel in my childhood or at the time I was reading her book. She talked about "finding one's pack,"[2] which opened up the possibility of relief and understanding that maybe there is some place where I can feel that I belong.

Her story about the Ugly Duckling brought tears to my eyes, and her narrative brought hope to my soul. She describes what it was like for the duckling when he finally found his family after he had spent difficult times in his search for others with whom he felt like he belonged. I resonated with this, as I spent my young adulthood wandering and searching for something that could not be defined.

You can see that, because of my early years, I came by the orphan character honestly. Although I was not an orphan in the sense that my mother was, I had an absent father and a mother who could not be present with or adequately mother me because of her early experiences. Nature, my friends and my grandmother became my escape and balms for my raw wounds. I always felt connected and knew I belonged when I was alone in the English countryside and I knew my friends liked to be with me. My childhood as recounted above set the stage for my entire life. It was the emotional mold that the clay had been poured into.

Notes

[1] Marion Woodman and Jill Mellick. *Coming Home to Myself*, p. 282.

[2] Clarissa Pinkola Estes. *Women Who Run with the Wolves*, pp. 166-198.

Personal Thoughts

I believe from my many experiences that the spirit world is more real, more solid, than this earth in which we live. In truth, ours is a world of illusion. All that seems so solid is yet just a mass: molecules locked together, forming an impression of solid matter that in fact is not solid at all.[1]

—Rosemary Altea
(used with permission of the author.)

3.
INTRODUCTION TO THE SPIRIT WORLD

Have you ever had an inner knowing about other worlds? Has something ever happened to you that made you question, "Is this all there is?" when you looked around the material world?

Part of my preparation for meeting Babaji seemed to be a strong connection that I had with the spirit world. I learned as a young child that different realms existed outside of this mortal world that I was born into and with which I was most familiar.

My introduction to the spirit realm came from my paternal grandmother, or my Nan, as I called her. Nan, together with my childhood friends, were calming balms on the wounds I inherited from my parents. I could walk to Nan's house, which was also not far from my junior school. I would spend many happy hours with her as she generously gave me food and love. The small coal fire in her living room was the focus of our relationship. We would sit on either side of the fireplace in overstuffed chairs and talk about all kinds of things. Dozing with her was a happy, contented pastime, too. This was interspersed with copious cups of hot tea.

One day, when I was seven or eight years old, she began to talk to me about a neighbor who had died. "I saw Mrs. Lee today," she said, looking at me with her steely blue eyes.

Initially confused, I said, "I thought Mrs. Lee had died."

"Yes, she died," was her response, "but I saw her looking at me through the kitchen window while I was doing the washing up."

I then went on to ask her what she looked like and whether she spoke to her, and I learned that Mrs. Lee was a frequent visitor to my grandmother. This left me with a matter-of-fact attitude and the knowledge that there was life after death and we can communicate with those who have crossed over to the other side. I never questioned this moving forward in my life, although I rarely talked about it to anyone. As young as I was, I knew instinctively that people didn't talk about these things, and I knew my parents would just tell me it was my vivid imagination.

But Nan was frequently in contact with another world. She was also able to receive information from living people at a long distance, using telepathy. There was one incident concerning my father. He was on one of his business trips to Brazil, but we had not heard from him in about three weeks. He was usually prompt, sending weekly letters to keep in touch. During these three weeks, Nan would ride to our house on her bicycle frequently, asking us whether we had heard from Dad.

This questioning would repeat itself, until finally, we received a letter telling us that Dad had been attacked by a German Shepherd dog and had to have stitches in his face. He recounted that he was lucky not to lose his eyesight. We explained this to Nan during her next visit, and she went deathly white and sat down. She said she had known there was something wrong with him because she had a dream in which she saw him with his arms at his side and blood pouring down his face. We later determined she had the dream at the exact time Dad had been attacked.

This was my introduction to the seriousness of dreams and the importance of giving them worthy attention. Little did I know that later in my life, I would study dreams in depth and offer dream exploration as an integral part of my work as a psychotherapist. Dreams would also be the medium that Babaji used to come into my life.

There was something very comforting to me as a child to sit around the fire having deep conversations with Nan about the mysteries of life. I remember gazing into the flames and being captivated by them as I listened to her. Maybe this was a meditative state and a precursor to my interest in meditation as an adult. I loved watching the red-hot coal and the patterns it would make as it burned away and slowly disintegrated into white ash. Periodically, a pattern of stars and sparks would be released. I was entranced. I did not know it then, but fire was to become an important symbol for me later in my life, as it connected me to the Divine, to myself and the whole of nature.

Those times of comfort with Nan and her fire provided some peace in my teenage years, when I was limping along with my life and coping the best way I could. Sitting with her transported me to a different world and gave me the renewed energy I needed to face the life I was living. I was unsure of myself and my abilities. I developed anxiety that would cripple me before my tests and exams. I was in a school for academic excellence that I hated and would never have survived if it hadn't been for my friends ,who provided humor and a sense of fun. They also shared their families with me, which became a necessary respite from the difficult relationship with my mother.

I was told by an English teacher in high school, "You are not academically inclined; you are the type who will be married before you are 20." This was in response to asking her if I could major in her subject. I was to prove her wrong about this, but it was an abusive and judgmental statement to make to a vulnerable 15-year-old who has not yet discovered her wings.

Life began to change for me when I was 16 and in my last year of high school. My dad had been working in Canada and had agreed to take a long-term position there, which would mean a move for the family. I absolutely did not want to go and preferred to stay behind and finish my high school year. It felt frightening to leave all my close friends and everything I had ever known to go and live in another country with my parents, who didn't feel like my family. Fortunately for me, my parents agreed, and plans were made for me to live with a friend.

Mum obviously had mixed feelings and would ask me on more than one occasion, "Do you want me to stay behind with you?" I was shocked by her question, because it seemed that she was carrying uncertainty about where her loyalty lay. In no uncertain terms, I told her that her place was with her husband and I would be able to manage on my own. I finally felt free as a bird that had suddenly been let out of a cage. I loved spending time with my friends and their families, and my life began to feel somewhat stable.

Even so, I was experiencing a growing sense of pressure, both inside myself and from my parents, to decide on my future. I remember my father, who was always practical, giving me words of advice: "You will never find what you are looking for, so you'd better find a nice boy and settle down." He was astute enough to realize I was looking for something, but it definitely was not a nice boy. I had a couple of semi-serious boyfriends in my teenage years, but I knew that marriage or a serious commitment was not what I wanted. It would take me many more years to find what eventually would lead me to what I was looking for.

I realize now that many fathers of his generation were scared to be raising a girl and could not wait for her to be married off so they would be relieved of further emotional and economic support. "Just hand her over to another man and I will be off the hook" was their mantra. Patricia Reis writes about this in her book, *Daughters of Saturn*. When writing about the personal father, she notes:

> *The culmination of his responsibility toward her (his daughter) takes place when he "gives her away" (as a virgin) in marriage to another man. . . . A daughter thus dependent moves from the "safety" of her father's house into the "security" of her husband's home . . . a woman's worthiness has been easily judged according to her ability (or lack thereof) to eventually find her way to this scenario.*[2]

How symbolic is that? It is also a vivid reminder of the power of the patriarchy and these examples we take for granted that are built into the underpinnings of society.

I think this may be truer for my generation and generations before mine than it is today, although we see today where young people are hesitant to leave the "father's house" and spend many more years of young adulthood there than did earlier generations.

Thankfully, I did not fall for this and was determined to forge an independent life. As a youngster, I was always considered willful by my parents. This was said as a judgment and felt like something of which I should be ashamed. I know that I knew things on a deep internal level and was not prepared to settle for anything less, even if it involved conflict, which it frequently did.

As I moved into my teenage years, the willfulness became rebellion. I think it was my way of hanging on to my spirit and not becoming completely lost in my environment. Neverthe-less, these two qualities would have to be revisited again as an adult to make sure that they were not used to sabotage my relationships, but rather, to enhance them.

It took me until my 40s to really understand that my dad's generation of men understood loving as being "a good provider." I heard this term so often when I was growing up. It was used as a high compliment for a husband. Being this way was how they demonstrated their love to their families. They did not understand this new generation of women who saw love as a heart-filled connection. These women knew they could care for themselves economically and they no longer needed a man to provide food and housing for them. They wanted something more.

At this young age, I knew I did not need a man, but I was always aware that I could not live peacefully with this ache and yearning I was carrying in my soul unless I was closer to understanding it. My father recognized a dissatisfaction in me, probably before I was even aware of it in myself. I have since learned to see it as a game of hide and seek when friends cry out "Warm!" as you draw closer and "Cold!" as you move away. It was as if I had an inborn sensor that could keep me on track, and when I felt I was getting closer, I was satisfied. If I was conflicted, knowing my sensor was not working, I would wait for a dream or some sign indicating which direction I should take.

Dad's statement has stayed with me, for I instinctively knew that his advice to find a young man was wrong for me. I did not know what I was looking for and could not put it into words at that age, but I knew I had to move forward on this strange path that was unfolding before me. Today, I know unequivocally that if you don't pursue what you are looking for, you will never find it. Dad was telling me to settle for something less—and that I could not do.

Notes

[1] Rosemary Altea, Azquotes, last accessed February 13,2021, (Altea n.d.). Used with permission of the author.

[2] Patricia Reis, *Daughters of Saturn*, New York: Continuum Publishing Co. p. 30. Used with permission of the author.

Our banquet of dreams is spread each night.
We can choose to eat.
We can choose not to eat.[1]

—Coming Home to Myself
by Marion Woodman and Jill Mellick: Conari Press

4.
ENTERING THE DREAMING WORLD

Two nights ago, I went to bed and asked for a dream to help me adequately and simply convey the psychological impact that dreams have on our path toward transformation. In my dream, I saw an ancient oak tree that had been recently felled. The stump was enormous and held its face proudly to the heavens. On further inspection, I noticed the numerous bands, alternating light and dark, that circled around the entire inside of the trunk. I was awed and mesmerized by this picture.

This was initially puzzling. Why had the dream world shown me a picture of a felled oak tree to symbolize the psychological importance of dreams? I then realized the similarities between us as human beings and this majestic tree. The bands within her trunk indicate the number of years she has been alive. They tell the story of her life experience in a way that is difficult to understand, for we do not know what is stored there. It is significant that this is only revealed to us after she is dead.

From the outside, as she is living, no one would ever know the rich history she carries inside. We humans are much the same, but we have discovered that we are lucky enough to have access to this knowledge while we are alive, through our dream world. As the tree stump presents a picture of her history, so our dreams present a collection of pictures of our inner world or psyche. It also connects us to the consciousness of the entire cosmos.

We are all connected to ourselves and each other through this astonishing world of dreams. They provide daily snapshots of how our inner world is responding to the events of the day. These are presented in pictures like the image of the oak tree. As we spend time with the images, they begin to speak to us and inform us at a deep level. They ultimately provide guidance and help us to resolve conflict, avoid danger, understand our blind spots, change our perception of ourselves and get to the truth of who we really are. They vastly expand our lives.

Today as a dream therapist, I guide countless people through their dreams as they begin to understand how their background and history impact their lives today. With this knowledge, they are able to make different decisions and to restructure how they see themselves.

In the early 60s, none of this knowledge was available to me, but because of my talks with my grandmother and my growing knowledge of the spirit world, I developed an interest in dreams. Nan had illustrated to me how loved ones can communicate with us through our dreams when she shared how she had come to know Dad had an accident while he was abroad.

I felt a pull to know more. This was a world I wanted to explore. What was the connection between my dreams and this spirit world that Nan introduced me to? I could sense that my grandmother was reticent to answer my questions about her experiences, and I appreciated her caution because she had already talked about happenings I knew to be off limits for the average person. The whole subject was a secret between us, and I knew I couldn't push her. She was also quite superstitious, so there is no telling what she thought might happen if she were to divulge too much of what she knew. She lived in a time when knowledge of another world held a stigma and was often related to witchcraft.

That stigma is the reason that psychic experiences are not talked about today. They can be disguised by contemporary terms such as *mystic* or *medium*, but the relics of the old term linger for generations in the psyche.

Since those early years, dreams have played a significant role in my life, and I have studied to better understand the symbolic language with which they present themselves. In this nighttime show, we are the author and producer of the plot, as well as every character we meet along the way. The dream often balances the unconscious and conscious worlds. For example, if we consciously try to live in the light and tend to look at everything positively, our dreams may reveal shadow qualities. It was a shock to me when I learned that our conscious mind takes up only 20% of our total psyche. The other 80% is unconscious . We function from an awareness that is only 1/5 of the totality of our psyche. This means that we make many decisions based on what we are carrying in our unconscious and they may or may not be helpful to us. We are operating with a very limited view of ourselves, the world and the cosmos.

Dreams frequently contain people we judge negatively in our waking lives, and this is an invitation to ask ourselves, "What is it about this person I do not like?" Since every person in a dream represents an aspect of us, we have an opportunity to look for this quality in ourselves so we can come to terms with it. As my grandmother taught me, there are also telepathic dreams (the ability to communicate with other people) and visitation dreams. Jung never talked about or really identified the latter type, although he was known to dabble in psychic phenomena. A visitation dream is a visit from a loved one who has passed to the other side. It announces itself by the level of energy we experience when we wake up. People have told me that they dreamed of a deceased family member "and it was so real, exactly as if he were there." There is frequently communication and a message that they relay to us.

The first significant dream I ever had came to me at this challenging time in my life after my parents had moved to Canada. While I was happy with my living situation, I faced inner and outer pressure to make some decisions about my future. I was flying back and forth to visit my parents in Canada, at the same time half-heartedly thinking about my future in England. I was in a limbo of sorts, and I knew it could not continue. I was intrigued by Canada as a new adventure, but I didn't want to leave the friends I had grown up with, and especially my grandmother. I did not miss my parents at all, but there was a part of me that wondered whether my place was with them, since they were my immediate family. I was conflicted, and as a result, frozen into a place of indecision.

This was to change quickly while spending the summer with my grandparents and working a temporary job. I had the following life-changing dream.

I am taking a walk in the woods, and I am without care. Enveloped by stately trees and overgrown vegetation, I am following no particular path—just the easiest way to navigate the lush green density.

Suddenly, I stop in my tracks as I enter a natural, barren clearing. It is startling to my eye. Where am I? What is this place where Mother Nature in her full greenery fears to tread? I am aware of a tense knot in the pit of my stomach. How can I tread where the earth's benefactors refuse to go?

I move slowly and cautiously forward to the middle of the clearing, and I notice two distinct paths leading out. "What shall I do now? Which way shall I take?" I ask myself. Of course, I can always retrace my steps and go out the same way I came in, but that does not even occur to me.

Studying the first route, I realize that it looks similar to the trail that had just deposited me in this strange dell. The foliage is the same, but the trail is a little wider and the ground well-worn and trodden down by travelers who have gone before me. I look intently at the second one and notice, not far off, a fire that is beginning to burn the vegetation. Now, pressed into action by a sense of urgency, I make a swift decision. I will take the fiery path because I can see clearly what is ahead for me. I know what I am dealing with. It is also the most difficult path to take. The other path represents more of the same, and there may be trouble ahead that I cannot prepare for.

Taking off at a run, I can feel the heat and suffocation as I zigzag between falling tree limbs and avoid persistent tongues of fire that are not yet ravaging. With raw and heavy lungs and aching legs, I slow to an easy pace as I realize that the fire is now far behind me. I now walk for what seems like an eternity. I am lost and in an unfamiliar place, but surprisingly, not scared.

Suddenly, the landscape changes again as I enter a grassy field with the ground covered in wildflowers as far as the eye can see. The colors are bright and intense, a mixture of blues and yellows contrasted, yet in harmony with the greenness of the meadow and the blueness of the sky. It is beautiful, and I feel my *soul sing as I begin to run in this Monet-inspired composition with arms outstretched and a feeling of total freedom and joy.*

I awoke with a start, and for a moment, felt totally disoriented and unaware of my surroundings. This dream was so real, and I could still feel the pounding in my chest and the sense of joy and exhilaration in my heart. I could still see the vibrant flowers and feel the breath of the breeze upon my face. It filled me with a desire to experience this moment again and again. I had never dreamed as vividly, and it seemed hugely significant and a portent of my life to come.

I slowly returned to the physical reality of laying in bed in my grandparents' spare bedroom. I lay there for some time enjoying the remnants of the dream and thinking about its possible meaning.

I then realized what I had to do.

Recalling this dream more than 50 years later, I am noticing even more how symbolic and relevant it was for me at that time. The path represents my life's journey and my spiritual path. In the beginning of the dream, I was wandering aimlessly with no particular direction. Then I found myself in a clearing (my grandparents' house), where I could get some clarity and space to decide on my future. The dream indicated there were two options open to me. One was to take the well-trodden road that had been taken by many people. For me it symbolized a route that might have been taken by the collective or my parents and grandparents before them. I knew that 30 years hence, I might be living in the same town with the same people, doing the same things. It would be a life of comfort, but also monotony, as I followed the same norms that had been laid down by generations ahead of me. The other route, however, indicated that I would face immediate challenges (the fire), but then experience the freedom and joy that came to me in the dream.

I had never felt these feelings before, but they resonated with my heart and soul, and I immediately knew that I had to take the path of fire and move to Canada.

Dreams frequently come with an inner feeling of "knowing" something. It is not a thought or an idea that originates in the head, but more of a gut feeling of instant recognition. This inner knowing or intuition can be developed over time, and once trusted, can be a reliable compass that guides us through challenging times.

Dreams are as unique to individuals as DNA and fingerprints. I instinctively knew that I had to take the route that seemed the most difficult. Others having the same dream might be convinced that they were being guided to take the easier path. The fire in this dream and the idea of walking a path of fire was to become very symbolic for me. When we look at the symbols in dreams, we must understand the dreamer's associations. My association to fire was the memory of sitting with my grandmother in an almost hypnotic state. They were happy and comforting times of closeness, communion and peace. Another dreamer may have an association of destruction and loss because they lost a family member in a fire. These personal associations are of utmost relevance when trying to understand a dream. For me, the fire was mesmerizing and I was not scared; for the other dreamer, it might signal a time of trauma and grief.

I would not know it then, but fire would continue to play an important role in my outer life, as well as become a constant symbol in my inner life.

Notes

[1] Marion Woodman and Jill Mellick. *Coming Home to Myself*, p. 180.

PART 2

SETTING OFF ON THE JOURNEY

We live our lives in a comfort zone. Ask yourself, 'If I had the courage and it were not for fear, what would I change in my life right now and how would I change it?' Then take a leap of faith and JUST DO IT.

—Elaine Heroux

5.

NEW COUNTRY, NEW FRONTIER

For many of us, there are defining moments in our lives. Often, we can only see them when we look back from the vantage point of our older years. At the time, we are so engrossed in a situation that we cannot see clearly. It may be a moment when we take a risk or a leap of faith. It may happen when we know that at some level there is something missing, or that we are living with unhappiness or discomfort. Like the grit in an oyster, the internal conflict rubs against us until we take action toward creating a highly valued pearl of wisdom.

For me, the impetus came from a dream; for others, it may come from an invitation to walk through a different door. Some may be catapulted into a new awareness by a traumatic experience or deep loss. Some may just decide one day that they don't like their existing situation, so they make a conscious decision to leave a marriage or their country or the career they have been working in for years.

This decision takes courage and can result in different challenges, but it frequently leads to the discovery of the pearl of great price, which in this case is an authentic connection with oneself and the awareness of our very soul.

Moving to Canada from England was one of these times for me and one of the most difficult tasks of my life. I had spent 17 years living on the same street, surrounded by the same neighbors and going to the same school, and my friends had been with me all the way. Suddenly, I was in a completely different culture where the drinking age was 21 and children were not included in adult activities. I was still considered a child in Canada, whereas I had been living a responsible, adult life in the UK for at least two years. It felt like going back in time with no points of reference. I felt totally disconnected, and this validated my lifelong feelings of not belonging. This was another "outsider," experience as I struggled to find a way to fit into a very different world. I had spent my childhood attempting to cope with the world I had been born into, and I had been able to adjust to this—but now I was in an alien world in the form of a strange culture. I had lost the continuity with myself.

The comfort of knowing people I had grown up with was no longer there. The intimate knowledge of the Earth's contours as I ambled down country lanes was gone. I had moved from a place of freedom, love of friends and independence to a strange land where people could not walk from place to place or easily hop on a bus or train. I was untethered, adrift and completely lost. I was experiencing intense homesickness.

Homesickness is the ultimate feeling of not belonging. It is the grief of loss—not just the loss of one person or object, but the loss of everything you have ever known. It is the pulling away of the very ground you are walking on. It was too overwhelming to take in completely, like a flower that has been transplanted in a different garden and strange neighborhood, and is wilting under the stress. My roots were battered and bruised, and I wasn't sure I could make it. I needed nourishment, and there was little available. Feeling so agonizingly alone, I found myself reaching out to connect in ways that were dangerous and did not represent my deepest values. I became involved with a party group of my parents' friends where there was a great deal of drinking. I knew this was not what I wanted for myself, but I was lonely and wanted to fit in. I was miserable and floundering before I was 21 years old.

This initial experience of homesickness was the portent of a sense I would always carry. It was a growing awareness that my longing which was always just under the surface would take me into strange lands and pioneering experiences in an effort to find my home. It was the search for a lover whom I could melt into and dissolve with. I knew this was not a mortal lover, because a human could not satisfy this unquenchable thirst that I carried within. I know now that it was the birth of my spiritual journey and the search for the Divine Mother, who represented to me the mother I never had.

It was during this time of excruciating homesickness and the challenges of adjusting to a new country that I met a new friend and probably the first mentor in my life. She was to become a lifeline that was thrown to me as I bobbed and weaved through a stormy sea with no sight of land.

Veronica—or Von, as I called her—was the same age as my mother but completely different in many ways. Short and redheaded with an infectious laugh, she was a raging extrovert and had a great sense of fun. It was all of this but more so her feyness that attracted me to her. The Urban Dictionary defines a fey as a "mythical being, enchanted, strange and other-worldly." Von exhibited all these qualities to me, and we spent many hours in conversation about life and death and all subjects in between. Thankfully, she was a wonderful sounding board for me as I poured out my grief, sadness and confusion concerning my life.

Von had just joined the Spiritualist Church in Hamilton. At that time, and it still may be the case, Spiritualism was more popular in the UK and Canada than it seemed to be in the United States. It is a religion that believes in God and also in mediumship. Mediumship is a means for people to communicate with loved ones who have died and passed over to the other side, by communicating through a medium. At this young age, I had a fascination for the subject that was based on my conversations with Nan.

One day, Von invited me to a social gathering where she had also invited one of the mediums from the church. I went with mixed feelings. Part of me felt excited, but there was another part that felt scared. I realize now that when I was younger, the spirit world always presented itself to me with a mixture of elation and resistance. Maybe the resistance was fear of the unknown, or fear of being judged, or fear of unleashing negative actions in my life. The mixed feelings may have also been a battle between the ego and the Self. The excitement is there as a form of guidance, yet the ego feels threatened by this and wants to control the situation. I have learned that if this energy is present, I must walk through the fear because I am being called to something that is larger than I. As I think about this, I am aware of having the same feelings around writing this book. They have been with me for more than two or three years, and I frequently resort to procrastination.

To return to that memorable night, I had numerous questions: What will this man be like? Is he a fraud? How will this affect me? In retrospect, this was the first time in my life that my body would signal to me the portent of something that was to be enormously significant and indicate that a door was opening toward something profound. It was a state of supreme alertness signifying a new level of energy about to enter the body.

I don't remember much about the evening. I think it was a small group of people in Von's home. The man's name escapes me, but I can still remember him after all these years. He was a short, rotund man who seemed a little strange. He did not seem to be very socially adept. Sitting in a solitary chair, he was noticeably quiet and did not intermingle. People would go up to him and ask him questions, but I was giving him a wide berth and watching from afar.

Toward the end of the evening, he approached me, and with no preamble, said, "Your grandmother wants to visit you but does not want you to be scared. Is that OK with you?" I was stunned, as if suddenly struck by a taser. What did he mean by this? My automatic response was a nod, yes. My head was answering his question while the rest of my body was in a state of suspended animation. I knew instinctively that he was referring to my great grandmother, the mother of my beloved Nan. She had passed away a few years before this. Dismissing his words as I left for home was the only way I could deal with the question, as well as where my imagination might go if I allowed it to be unbridled. I had no framework that I could relate to except my grandmother's stories, which were, at that point, furthest from my mind. Everything was to be revealed two nights later.

I awoke with the sense that someone had sat down on the side of my bed. At that time, I was living alone in a small one-bedroom apartment, so this was impossible unless it was an intruder. However, I instinctively knew that I was safe. I looked to the right, where the pressure originated, and my great grandmother was standing there. I called her Granny. In life, she was a short, round woman of about 4'6". She wore white hair pulled back into a bun, and in her later years, walked quite slowly and laboriously in her black Mary Jane shoes. There was no question that she was standing next to me, but she looked different. Her skin was translucent, and although she looked as she did when she was older, she had a youthful appearance. She told me not to be scared and not to try and touch her. She had a lightness around her that must have lit up the room because I was able to see my room clearly, which wouldn't normally happen in the dark.

I began to talk to her, the words tumbling out of my mouth and falling over themselves. I asked her what it was like where she was, and this was her reply: "It is like a school where we learn all the time. When you die, you go into the level that you are at in your life. It's like many different classes, based on where you are when you cross over." She ended with the admonishment, "That's why you have to lead a good life, my girl, for you take yourself with you when you go." Those words have stayed with me my entire life.

I remember looking at the clock on the bedside table as she spoke. It was 1 a.m. I asked her if she had been to visit Nan in the same way, and she said she had. I then remember falling back to sleep without seeing her leave.

I woke again sometime later. I was in an elevated state energetically. I felt so happy and excited as I lay thinking about Granny. It was about this time that the doubts began to enter my mind and I asked myself, *What just happened? Was it a dream or was she really there?* At a very deep level, I knew it was real and the energetic buzzing of my body confirmed this fact, but I needed some kind of proof. If it was a dream, it was a dream within a dream because I distinctly remember waking up and going back to sleep. Normally, a dream has small details that indicate it comes from the imagination, but my room and its contents were exactly as they were in reality. I remembered the clock and decided I would check the time, which I remembered so clearly as I was talking to her. If the clock announced it was before 1 a.m., then I must have dreamed it. My room was now in its usual darkness, so I turned on the light and looked at the clock. It said 3 a.m. That meant I could not rule out that the experience was real. I decided to wait until the summer, when I would see Nan, and ask her whether she had a similar experience.

Sleep eluded me for the rest of the night because of the energy that was surging through my body. I wanted to shout out from the rooftops and tell the world that my Granny had come to visit me from the other side and told me what it was like there.

I was floating 12 inches off the ground as I prepared for work and arrived early to share my experience with my co-workers. Propelled by the high I was feeling, I did not stop to think about how my proclamation might be received. I waited until they had all arrived, and I told them. Their reaction was unforgettable. They literally looked at me in silence, and a pall fell over the room. Some of them took a step back, and others turned their bodies away. My energy and excitement plummeted, and I knew I had made a mistake. The unspoken messages that came to me thick and fast were that I was more than a little "strange," maybe even "mad" or "crazy." It was as if a huge sheet of thick ice had descended from the ceiling and now separated me from them. I was trapped behind the ice and knew I could not get out until I started talking and acting normally and in a way that was familiar and acceptable to them. It was never mentioned again.

I was more than scared. It was a paralyzing fear that emanated through the room, transforming something that was beautiful into an ugly alien experience that made me question my reality and that profoundly separated me from my co-workers. This was to become a frequent theme in my life as I managed to keep these instances hidden from others and stored carefully on the back shelves of my psyche.

In the outside world, I was functioning well and dutifully. I presented myself in ways that were expected of me and slid into the murky background of normality. I worked hard and had many friends. I never returned to the Spiritualist gatherings and rarely talked about this experience again, and certainly not in a public way, until now.

There was one exception. That same summer, I returned to England and told Nan what had happened. I asked her whether she had received a visit from Granny in a similar way. I looked into her penetrating blue eyes as the silence lengthened between us. She slowly nodded her head yes, and we never talked about it again. I'm not sure why this was never discussed, except that together with her reticence about sharing and my experience with my co-workers, we decided at a nonverbal level to keep these occurrences close to our chests. It was a huge validation for me, however, that what had happened was real and not a figment of my imagination.

This is what I call a visitation dream, because it involves a visit from someone who has passed away. In his *Collected Works*, Jung talked about the different types of dreams. Compensation dreams entail the psyche attempting to balance the unconscious with the conscious. In reductive compensation dreams, the psyche looks backwards toward repressed memories, whereas prospective dreams guide us into the future. Jung does acknowledge telepathy in dreams but never acknowledges that dreams may be a portal to another world.[1]

In recent years, I worked as a counselor in nursing-home and assisted-living settings. Once the residents learned to trust me, I heard from them of their visitations on an almost-daily basis. Many would share, in great detail, conversations they had with loved ones on the other side. They had no fear of dying because they knew they were preparing to be with their departed family members. The sadness for me is that traditional medicine and belief puts these experiences in the category of psychotic or delusional, and these seniors are never really heard and validated for talking about them.

Is it too difficult to imagine that reality is different for different people? Does that mean I am right and the other is wrong if we don't see things eye to eye? It is not culturally acceptable to acknowledge or talk about spiritual visitations, yet spiritual visitations are a reality for thousands of people. What would it be like if we learned to talk about our differences and celebrate them? Maybe we would understand autism, dementia and other conditions that are labeled as neurological problems in a different light. Maybe we would be freer to explore the ramifications of proving the existence of other worlds and realities. Perhaps we would even discover a new dimension that has previously been unknown to us as a species.

A few brave souls have experienced spiritual and creative breakthroughs in their sleep and have written about them. Dmitry Mendeleyev was a Russian chemist who lived in the 19th century. During a period of intense work, he went to bed and dreamed of an arrangement of elements that was to change modern chemistry forever. He saw a table of elements in its entirety, which he was able to capture on paper as soon as he awoke. This table contained all the known elements, as well as eight more that had not yet been discovered. Where did this information come from? An enquiring mind might ask that question, but all too often these instances are seen as oddities because they fall outside social and cultural norms.

If we look again more closely at the fabric of our lives, we may see that it is enriched with a strand of silver or gold, or a vibrant red that jumps out as it weaves itself over time. We may also notice quieter, more subdued colors that form the backdrop to our masterpiece. Upon further inspection, we notice some threads may be thicker than others and made of different material. Altogether, it creates a work of art that is unique and breathtaking in its beauty. The people around us have the same effect. They reflect parts of ourselves back to us.

They offer depth and character and added dimension, as well as love and companionship. The more diverse people are, the greater the understanding between them and the richer the relationships. If we learn to think outside the box, we can learn to treasure our differences and learn from them. We can begin to live in a multicolored, multifaceted world instead of one that is monochromatic.

Notes

[1] C.G. Jung, CW, Vol. 8, *The Structure and Dynamics of the Psyche*, pp. 260-261.

Personal Thoughts

In early adulthood we are creating a foundation for life whether we know it or not. Ask yourself what is important to you and build these values into your foundation.

—Elaine Heroux

6.
WORKING AND TENDING

Young adulthood is a time for digging and planting and tending and growth, and forms the foundation for many future years. It is the time for pursuing a career, settling down, maybe starting a family. It is different for everybody, but I do know it's a time for learning about the outer world and discovering and strengthening our value system.

So, what are our values and how do we acquire them? These seems like a basic questions, which, surprisingly, often young people cannot answer. What is important to you and what would you say are your most important values?

More and more, we are seeing around us people who seem not to live by some of the more traditional values, such as respect, compassion and acceptance of others. When I was a child, basic codes for living were taught in school through the Ten Commandments and these became the standards to live by. In current times, the Golden Rule of treating others as we would like to be treated, may be acceptable to more people.

Values are principles or unspoken rules that we have for ourselves that are important and sometimes form our passion for living. They help give meaning to life. They determine our actions and feed our souls. Many people devote their entire lives to supporting one or more of these inner principles. Our veterans exhibit patriotism, which is an example of this. Then there are the love and kindness shown by Mother Teresa and the peace that was taught by Mahatma Gandhi. Their lives became a tribute to what they loved and believed, and it was clear to all those who were in their presence.

Hopefully, our culture and our families teach us these important principles. and it is the responsibility of each one of us to consciously adopt or reject what works for us. The Ten Commandments are non-negotiable for many of us, but there are many more that can be examined and changed. This is an important process during the years leading to midlife.

It is imperative that we periodically assess whether we are living in alignment with these values. If we are not, we will feel some inner conflict or dissonance.

Sometimes, we are prodded to reject a rigid principle we have adopted unconsciously because it does not work for us. An example of this is staying in an abusive or intolerable relationship because of our belief that marriage is forever. We must constantly reassess these values as we face different situations. By doing this, we come to learn what is important to us and what makes us happy. We learn how to relate to people and how to honor and respect ourselves and these inner principles that are meaningful to us. I'm not sure we all do this consciously, and we often learn the hard way. We sometimes understand our values by looking at what does *not* work for us. A failed marriage or a failed career tells us it's okay to fail and asks that we look for the gold in the lesson learned.

During the time I was exploring the spiritual world, I began to explore the emerging new computer world. I was living with my parents in an uncommunicative environment, and I did not know how to feel a belonging to the outside world. We lived on the top floor of an apartment building, and our days were dominated by a TV that was the focal point in our existence. I was miserable and spent almost all my time in my bedroom. My dad was the person who finally encouraged me to learn about computers. He convinced me that they were the "wave of the future" and would have enormous impact on the world. It was not something that really appealed to me, but in order to make friends and find a way to fit in, I signed up for a two-year associate degree program at a local college.

This was obviously not the best reason to start a career, but I was following Dad's values and advice about doing something that would provide a good and stable income. At this point, I had no idea about what I would really like to do and what would make me happy.

The course was the first of its kind and was in data processing. It started out with a class of 50 students, and by graduation there were 15 of us—and only 3 of us were women. I was a forerunner of the women's liberation movement and frequently found myself within the sphere of the masculine. I guess I was more comfortable there because I was able to relate better to men than to most women my age. This was another byproduct of my early years, in which my interactions and connections with my dad were stronger than those with my mother.

I realize now that because of my father, I aligned with the internal masculine principles more than my feminine. These were inner values centered around the importance of success in the world, a strong work ethic, independence and a love of freedom. My feminine was severely wounded by the poor relationship I had with my mother, and I had little desire to follow in her footsteps. This would lead me to an unconscious search for the feminine, but a feminine to whom I could easily relate.

Pursuing computers was another pioneering step in an area that was, at that time in 1967, undiscovered. Computers were relatively unheard of in the 60s, and like animals in a zoo, they were enormous creatures housed in environments that had to be carefully monitored to make sure they didn't overheat. It was difficult to communicate with these monsters because they spoke different languages from us and required us to spend tedious hours clarifying instructions and then typing them up on special cards. The cards were numbered in sequence and then fed into their mouths. If we were lucky, they would understand what we were telling them and respond appropriately to the instructions. Frequently, it would take time and many changes to get them to get the results we were looking for, and this could wreak havoc on our working world if we accidentally dropped a box of these cards and had to try and put them back in the same order.

There was a well-known mantra that was born in relationship to these artificial structures: "Garbage in, garbage out," or GIGO. If we fed them garbage, they would produce garbage. It caused us programmers to be very linear and critical in our thinking and to allow for all hidden responses that we may have missed. It would seem that the spiritual world would be light years away from this world of new technology, yet I am struck by the similarity of concepts. As humans, we are only as functional as the messages we received as children that were handed down through generations. The spiritual path requires mindfulness and curiosity in order to understand the messages we have been fed and the persistence and courage to change them to get new and different results. GIGO became an important mantra for me as I moved through adulthood, learned to take responsibility for my life by examining my thoughts and beliefs, and monitored my responses and actions to difficult situations.

When I was 27, I met my future husband. At this point, I had become quite disillusioned with men and had focused my energy on my work and many friends who were single and married, male and female. I had been carrying a torch for an

English man with whom I worked, but he had ended the relationship but kept up a friendship of sorts. I think I was still holding out hope that he would come to his senses and take steps toward rekindling the connection we had. I was not interested in starting over with another man. I felt I had the best of all worlds when I was invited to a Sunday dinner with married friends, went out for an evening with single friends or lived with a family whose children became like my children. I was quite satisfied and comfortable with my life and did not expect any interruptions.

Tom had one strike against him before we even met in that he was introduced to me by my mother. My parents were now living in Kansas, and we would get together once a year for a vacation. For some time, my mother had considered me "way too old" to be single, and her raison d'etre was to find me a man. Tom was her third attempt at matchmaking. She arranged for a family weekend in Las Vegas and said, "Oh, by the way, I have invited Tom to come along, too." I was disgusted and opposed to this decision, which was made with no input from me. I firmly advised her that since she had invited him, she could entertain him, as I wanted nothing to do with the man. The strikes against him were already piling up, and I hadn't even met him.

The weekend started off shakily with me refusing to sit with him in the front seat of the rental car in which he had driven to meet us. "Aren't you going to sit in the front seat with Tom?" my mother gushed as she attempted to throw us together.

"No thank you, I'll sit in the back," I responded as I climbed as gracefully as I could into the back seat of the car. I noticed he wore a huge grin on his face; he was not fazed by my rudeness, and in fact, he thought it funny. At that point I thought that maybe he wasn't too bad, after all. By the end of the weekend, we both felt as if we had known each other our entire lives.

I know I resisted him and was even rude to him because my mother had introduced me to him. I was indignant that she would continue to try and control me and plan my life, and I couldn't imagine that I would like any man she would like. During that first evening, I saw Tom for who he was. He was his own man, and he had a great sense of humor. He was not easily intimidated. We talked for hours and learned that we shared a love of books and reading. He seemed to know his way around the outside world and was comfortable in his own skin. We were able to talk easily and effortlessly, and there was always something new to talk about. We could also be in a comfortable silence together. I felt as if I already knew him.

I often think about the story of the giant on the top of a hill, patiently cutting oranges in half and rolling them down the hillside. It is said that these halves represent two people, and when you find your match, you know it by the way you fit together. I don't know where I heard that, but the image stays with me because it seems appropriate for my relationship with Tom.

The big test for me was whether Tom was a man of his word. I had been disillusioned and disappointed so often by men that I was hyperalert to being lied to or promised something that would not be delivered. But Tom never, ever said he would do something without following it up. If he said he would call at 8 p.m. on a Saturday, I could rely on the call at that time.

For three months he commuted between Memphis, where he was living, and Canada every weekend. Since these were winter months, he would find himself snowed in at Pittsburgh airport en route and would finally arrive late Saturday before he would have to leave the next day. At Christmas, we became engaged, twice—since I refused the ring on Christmas day but finally accepted it the following day. It was a difficult decision for me to agree to marriage because I had been alone and independent for so long. I didn't question him, but I did question myself. Would I be a good enough wife? Could I deal with marriage and a possible move? All my insecurities, which I had been trying so hard to overcome, were once more in my face in an alarming way. Tom's response was perfect for me. He assured me that it would not work if I had doubts and maybe we needed to split up. This gave me the freedom to make the commitment. Had he tried to pressure me in any way, I would have moved on.

I realize now that the qualities I saw in Tom were those I could not see in myself because they were so poorly developed or disowned. Tom became the outspoken rebel that was missing in me. One who was not afraid to speak his own truth, whether or not others agreed with him. One who could be sacrilegious at times and could cut through any BS that was offered. He grounded me when my head was in the clouds.

I moved to Memphis in January, and we were married in March. As the saying goes, the rest is history.

I had moved to a third country in 27 years, and I was ready to begin a new chapter in my life.

You can never cross the ocean until you have the courage to lose sight of the shore.[1]

—Andre Gide

7.
CONFRONTATION WITH ROLES

Carl Jung uses the metaphor of the Sun to describe his views on the stages of life.[2] He sees our early adulthood as a time of working and growing; this stage is geared toward achievement and rewards, and successfully fitting in with society. The second half of life is more about introspection, assessing the past and finding meaning. The goal of the first half is to build a strong ego while the goal of the second half is to be able to transcend the ego.

Once again, I found myself in a different culture with no friends. The newness of this transition was helped enormously by my husband. The next 15 years marked a relatively quiet time of adjusting to marriage and being a stepmother to Tom's 9-year-old son. I would say it was quiet from the outside, but there were also many inner challenges.

These years in Memphis were an ego-building, practical time for me. I always worked, but now I had a husband and stepson to consider. Finding your way as a stepparent is always challenging, and I knew that I did not want children of my own until I learned to love my stepson. When I finally achieved that, I did not feel the need to have my own children, and I questioned my ability to be a good enough mother to a new infant after my experiences with my own mother.

Being a stepmother was unknowingly an invitation for me to explore a relationship outside the normal established roles. I knew I could never replace my new son's mother, nor would I have wanted to. I did want to have a relationship with him and to build a mutual trust and affection, ultimately leading to love. This had to be done on a part-time basis on weekends and with his mother still in the picture. It was not always easy, but I initially focused on building trust and stepping back, as he reclaimed some of the connection he had had with his father before the divorce. I found myself constantly thinking about how I could best help them. This meant sometimes getting involved, but mostly watching from the sidelines. This triggered many of my earlier memories of feeling as if I didn't belong.

The idea of roles was my biggest hurdle. Suddenly, I found myself in the positions of wife and stepmother, and deep down I felt I was ill equipped to handle them. For me, roles signified acting and complacency, and were far removed from independence and authenticity. How could I juggle these responsibilities and be true to myself at the same time? How does one balance this new position while grasping at, and desperately trying to hold on to, her most precious values? It was difficult at times as I tried to hang on to myself while I feared drowning in a sea of chores and expectations.

Patricia Reis addresses this in *Daughters of Saturn*:

The desire for relationship and the desire to be fully oneself are frequently pitted against each other. Both desires imply a certain kind of abandonment: in one the woman abandons herself to a man, in the other, to "the open channels" of herself. . . . The effort to be autonomous is difficult because it runs counter to all that women have been taught. . . . To remove oneself, to separate from another's needs in order to create, is thought of as selfish at best and monstrous at worst. It is so much more acceptable and rewarding to be "good." 3

I did not realize it at the time, but this was the conflict that was unconsciously raging inside me, leaving me feeling inadequate and anxious. My willfulness thankfully rose to the occasion, and I was determined not to just flop into these roles without giving them some thought. I knew there was more to life than this, and I was determined to find it.

Something I am grateful for is that I always worked and saw this as one way I could keep the tenuous connection I had built with myself. Through work, I was able to retain a certain independence, and at the same time, it placed me in an outside arena where I was meeting people and could be seen for who I was as a professional and a person.

I realize now that I had entered this state of holy matrimony with no guidance except the unspoken modeling by my parents of what a marriage should look like. My parents had a traditional marriage in which my dad was the breadwinner, and my mum was a stay-at-home mother. Mum did the baking, cleaning and laundry, and cared for me—that was her "job," while Dad traveled to exotic countries and made sure that money was deposited in the bank. Since Dad was my idol as a child and the idea of far-away lands seemed so alluring, I knew on some level that his was the life I wanted to emulate. I couldn't see myself living in a garden of domesticity.

At the time of my marriage, I was not consciously aware of any of this and I blindly followed in my mother's footsteps, thinking, *This is what I have to do to be a good wife*, and, *This is how it is meant to be*. I knew I was not feeling fulfilled, and resentments began to smolder under the surface. Persisting with my career, however, was one way I had broken the mold that had been set by my family of origin.

There were many happy memories that eased some of the stress, and I loved the fact that our home was often the place where the neighborhood kids would hang out. Being an only child, I had often craved the company of other children, and for some reason, our home was frequently a hub of activity. I also have treasured memories of playing racquetball and golf as a family and finally feeling some sense of belonging.

My parents had moved to Memphis in the same year Tom and I were married, so these years were also a time of mending some of the fences from the past with them. It was the only time I lived around my parents since leaving home. Tom and I had a standing joke that every time I moved to live closer to my parents, they would move on to another state. This happened so many times, it was no longer funny and led to a resignation that I really was intended to live my own life, make my own decisions and not be included in my family of origin. Unknown to him, this permission to be free was one of the most precious and enduring gifts that my father had passed on to me.

Mum and Dad lived about ten minutes away from us and I would visit them every week, usually on a Sunday. This was a generational habit, since I remember visiting Nan every Sunday with my dad. Sometimes Tom would come with me, but more often I would go alone.

Occasionally, I would take Mum shopping during the week and we would spend the day at the mall. Our relationship was civil and quite different from how it was during those early childhood years. I think we had come to an unspoken truce. I had come to a realization that we would never be able to speak the same language, so I stopped trying to connect at a level that would have been more satisfying to me. I would listen to her and not argue as I did so many years before. I wanted a peaceful connection to her, and I felt like I paid a price for this. It was another example of how I wrapped my true self away in a cocoon from which I would not emerge for many more years.

My father worked until he was 80 years old, so Mum was alone in the daytime. She had friends and learned to golf, but she never learned to drive. We celebrated holidays together, and from the outside, it seemed we were a happy family. However, I was still carrying the wounding from my past and felt there was a huge gulf between us that couldn't be bridged. I did not know it then, but I was carrying enormous resentment and anger toward her, which was quietly seething below the surface.

I was to learn that healing childhood wounds is a long, slow process, and after my meeting with Babaji, I explored my wounds in a deeper, more intentional way.

Notes

[1] Andre Gide, Goodreads, last accessed February 13, 2021, (Buechner 1977) goodreads.com/quotes/192564, (Gide n.d.)

[2] Leslie Sawin, Lionel Corbett and Michael Carbine, editors, *Jung and Aging*, p. 10. Used with permission of the author.

[3] Patricia Reis, *Daughters of Saturn*. pp. 89-90. Used with permission of the author.

What if everything you see is more than what you see—the person next to you is a warrior and the space that appears empty is a secret door to another world? What if something appears that shouldn't? You either dismiss it, or you accept that there is much more to the world than you think. Perhaps it is really a doorway, and if you choose to go inside, you'll find many unexpected things.[1]

—Shigeru Miyamoto

8.
MORE EXPERIENCES OF THE SPIRIT WORLD

My spiritual life was on sabbatical during the first few years of my marriage. I never attended church or really thought much about a spiritual life. I think I was too busy working and trying to negotiate a domestic life. Functioning in the home and in the world were my priorities.

There were, however, two contacts with the spirit world that were memorable.

Tom and I were vacationing in England one summer and were taken to the Yorkshire Dales for a long weekend by my uncle and his wife. They had been going to this area of Yorkshire for many years and had fallen in love with it. They wanted to introduce us to the old disused tin mines they had discovered. We stayed in a small village that was typical old English. It consisted of one main street and a village green that ran through the center of the street, with an obelisk or market cross that represented its early influence as a market town. There was one pub on the street and a tiny village shop that also acted as a post office. The street was a few hundred yards long, so everything was within walking distance. The street was flanked by miniature stone cottages that looked as if they had been built in the late 18th century.

It was all a perfect representation of a Hallmark card scene or the porcelain villages that appear under the tree at

Christmas. To give you some idea of the size of this community, the census in 1901 indicated little more than 370 residents. The village grew rapidly from 1450 to 1750 and was a thriving market town, as well as home to the miners and stone quarriers who worked in the surrounding hills.

We stayed in one of the old cottages that faced the village green. It was a small, two-up and two-down house. Even with the warmth of midsummer, the coldness of the bricks could not be denied. From the minute I walked into the house, I felt depressed. This was not an emotional depression, but rather, a sense of drudgery and oppression. I woke up the first morning and could see men clustered around the table downstairs and preparing for the day. I imagined a stream of workers walking out to the tin mines for another day of excruciating, back-breaking work. It was a world of poverty and tedium.

These images were so real to me, it was almost as if I had been there in person and lived that life. Was I one of those miners in a previous incarnation? I will never know, but I do know the enormous impact this visit made on me. I have never mentioned this to anyone. It has been filed away in a storage file marked *secret and private.*

The second incident happened at a golf tournament in North Carolina. My husband and I had gone for a long weekend to play in a couples' tournament. We stayed in an elegant, large Georgian-style home that had been converted to a hotel. The building dated back to 1921. We had a beautiful room that contained two single beds. In the middle of the night, I woke up suddenly and watched as a nurse walked through the wall to my left. She walked along the bottom of the beds and kneeled at the side of my husband's bed, which was to my right. As you can imagine, I freaked out. By this time, she had disappeared into thin air. I woke my husband up urgently and told him what had happened. I was scared and concerned about going back to sleep. I jumped into his single bed, and we both slept scrunched up together for the rest of the night.

The following morning, I asked the front desk if the building had ever been a hospital. I was told that it had never been a hospital, but it was used temporarily as one during the war and housed veterans who had returned with injuries. That information gave me a sense of peace, and I realized that I had somehow tapped into an earlier time period.

That experience reminds me of an experience I had many years ago when I woke up one morning and knew that time was not linear. I don't know how I knew, but it was a fact. Something that happened to me before I awoke left me knowing without a shadow of a doubt.

As we evolve, it makes sense that we can tap into other times, either in the future or in the past. Nonlinear time means we can communicate with people who have gone before and those whom we have never consciously met, because we are living everything at the same time. Our brains are currently not wired in a way that can understand this. If we believe in reincarnation, maybe a previous life is not a previous life but a parallel life we are sensing at some level. There is another dimension we cannot fully comprehend, but we can see glimpses of it and learn to weave it into our belief systems. There may be more than one dimension.

Both aforementioned incidents could be described this way. I was sensing something from another time, and it presented itself into my current linear reality.

I have learned that knowledge of this other world does not signify that I am on a spiritual path. It has just proven to me over time that there is another world, and there are times when I am in contact with it. It has been part of my spiritual journey, but it is not the entire path. My knowledge of this world paved the way for meeting Babaji. I was open to experiences of the spirit world, even if they were sometimes scary to me.

It is important for me to finally share these secrets from my past. Secrets are the source of personal shame. By not talking about these spiritual happenings, I felt ashamed of them and believed I was defective in some way. This led to more isolation and increased separation from my peers. How would people understand these things? Would they think I was weird or crazy?

These are questions I have asked myself for my entire life. In many ways, these connections with the spirit world, and specifically, my meeting with Babaji have been the focal point of a life I have felt necessary to keep secret.

Is that what I want my legacy to be? A life of secrecy and shame? It is by sharing this life that I am finally recognizing what a gift it has been to me.

I also decided to share them because of something that happened last summer. I had a conversation with a young woman, Azelia, who confided that she sees dead people and has had spiritual visions. She is the daughter of beloved friends of mine, and I have known her since she was about nine years old. She is now in her mid-20s and is lovingly called my adopted granddaughter. Her mother told me this has been happening for her since she was very young. As a child, she was unable to sleep, so they sought help but never mentioned her visions to doctors. As an adult, she has been dealing with some anxiety.

Azelia explained to me that on more than one occasion, she saw somebody at work or in a private home but then didn't see them again. She asked a co-worker about the older pharmacist who was working with her. When she described him to the co-worker, she was told he used to work there but was now deceased. At another time, she went to a private home with her family and spoke to an older man who was sitting in the hallway. There was a picture of this man on the wall in the living room. As the evening wore on, she asked where he was, and she was told that he was no longer living. Her life was peppered with stories such as this.

She told me that only her closest family knew about it and explained how different she felt from her peers, as well as the difficulty she experienced in social situations. As I spoke with her, I was aware of how much she reminded me of myself when I was her age. I began to wonder how my life might have been different if I had met a mentor or guide who could have validated my experiences and helped me see them as enormous gifts. While my grandmother gave me a certain level of acceptance, it was obvious that she was not comfortable talking about it, either. Like me, this young woman could only see her experiences as burdens that caused her to feel separate from other people.

Close to the same time I spoke with her, I had another conversation with her mother and a group of women I have known for 15 to 20 years. We began to talk about this phenomenon of seeing people who have passed to the other side. To my astonishment, almost every woman present had had a paranormal experience.

Why had they never talked about this before? I should have known, because I too was afraid of sharing my contacts with the spirit world. I think women are more susceptible to these otherworldly connections because their feminine essence is receptivity, which makes them more open at a sensory and intuitive level. This does not mean that men with a highly developed feminine function are not able to have such experiences. I believe the interactions come through the feminine side, whether we are in in a male or female body.

Our culture fears the unknown, and that is why there are some subjects that cannot be discussed. The world also values left-brain thinking and science to the point that experiences are not "real" unless they can be backed up by science. Paranormal experiences fall squarely into this category. Throughout history there are numerous examples of women meeting an untimely and horrible death because they were accused of witchraft. The stigma that came out of the Salem witch trials in the 17th century is one example of this. Thus, women keep these phenomena to themselves because they know that if they speak up, they will become a lightning rod for ridicule and judgement. The subject of death is treated the same way. Nobody knows for sure what the afterlife is like, and some people cannot even accept that there is an afterlife because it has not been proven.

Many indigenous cultures have a complete philosophy and understanding of both worlds and work within that context, which is accepted and revered by the whole tribe. How would it be for us if this was the case in the world in which we live?

Now is the time for us to be open about this phenomenon and to share our experiences, which are begging for under-standing and acceptance. Secrets that we keep about anything prevent us from being whole and reaching our utmost potential. We are being urged to accept all aspects of ourselves and other people so we can heal the stigma and shame that have held us back for many generations. That is not to say it is an easy process. It is often long and painful, and we are required to stay grounded in the outside world as we traverse the memories, truths and misconceptions in our inner world. I believe we need a guide or guides who can help us with this.

Since my personal secrets revolved around my experiences of the spirit world, that is the perspective I am writing about. The same applies to secrets related to body trauma, such as physical abuse, rape and incest. Trauma of any kind has serious consequences for the individual and healing requires knowledge of its symptoms. This can be provided by a trained trauma therapist, preferably someone who has walked the same path.

For all secrets, whether about the spirit or the body, it is only when we claim our own truth that we can understand how the most devastating challenges we have faced in our lives contribute the most to our inner strength and enable us to look back and help those going through similar experiences. We are then able to fully explore life and contribute to our understanding of what it is to be both human and Divine at the same time.

We are continually evolving as humans, and the veil between different worlds is becoming more and more delicate. It is my belief that we are evolving into light beings who will eventually be able to cross and re-cross the veil at will. We can only contribute consciously to this evolution if we are prepared to celebrate our uniqueness and talk about it.

As we embark on our unique inner journey, it has been my experience that the further we travel inward, the more we discover parts of ourselves that are different from those of the culture in which we live—sometimes radically so. Because we fear other people's reactions, we are unable to see them as gifts and they become as yokes around our necks.

What would it be like if we could openly share and be respected for these differences? How would it change our lives if we could freely claim and explore our gifts in a public way? For me, I think I would have felt as if I had belonged to my community and my world from a young age. I would have thought I was making a contribution, and my self-esteem would certainly have been better.

Taking this inner journey to wholeness is more crucial now than it ever was. The world of technology, social media and 24-hour news has resulted in reducing the entire world so that we are constantly bombarded with images and news from far and wide. If you notice, the art of conversation and listening is declining and we are reduced to memes and mantras, resulting in little time for patience and tolerance of other people, as we live in a world of instant gratification. We can now be bullied and shamed on social media in a way we could never have imagined 60 years ago. This means we are pressured more and more to fall in line with current talking points.

Staying grounded and centered today takes courage and requires knowing ourselves well and seeing ourselves clearly. There are many tools available that will help us stay centered in our truth. These may include bodywork, yoga, meditation, nature and music. We are more likely to get caught up in the tsunami of images and loud messages if we do not know our own strength and weaknesses and cannot see our gifts or know our own inner values and how important they are.

Notes

---

[1] Shigeru Miyamoto, Goodreads, last accessed February 13, 2021, goodreads.com/quotes/360610 (Miyamoto n.d.)

PART 3

BABAJI ARRIVES

To reach the Goal you have to be turned inside out, burned with the fire of Love, so that nothing should remain but ashes, and from the ashes will resurrect the new being, very dissimilar from the previous one. Only then can there be real Creation. For this process is destruction, creation AND Love. Another name for Love is Pain and Effort.[1]

—From *Daughter of Fire*, by Irina Tweedie

9.
HOW BABAJI CAME INTO MY LIFE

As I mentioned before, I have been a pioneer, an explorer and a seeker for as long as I can remember. As a young child, I had questions about everything and could never be satisfied with the answers that came back to me. Frequently, the questions were dismissed entirely, which left me feeling as if I myself had been tossed away like an empty soda bottle. I knew that I had to find my own answers to these difficult questions.

Later, when I was 17 years old and leaving high school, I was in a state of confusion, as all my friends had serious boyfriends and were contemplating marriage and motherhood. I had no idea what I wanted and had yet another outsider moment in which I felt excruciatingly lonely and different from all my peers. I would ask myself: *What is wrong with me that I don't have a boyfriend and I have no desire to marry and have children yet?*

Somewhere deep inside of me, there was an ache or a longing that could not be described. I just knew it could not be quelled by another human being and that once I found what I was looking for, I would recognize it immediately. In retrospect, I have always been propelled more by knowing what I didn't want than by understanding what I did want. I would eventually find what I was looking for when I was 44 years old.

Still searching, I had been in an Association of Research and Enlightenment (ARE) Study Group for about five years. ARE was established by the psychic medium Edgar Cayce in 1931 and was dedicated to teachings about holistic health, ancient mysteries, dreams and reincarnation. These teachings were offered with a view to helping people with their lives. Cayce was also known as the Sleeping Prophet and would go into a trance-like state to recommend healing tips to those who were suffering from physical ailments.

The study group in which I found myself consisted of six to eight people who met on Sunday evenings to study Cayce's two volumes on *A Search for God*. One specific lesson was read during the week and discussed in the group. We then spent about 20 minutes in meditation. I was drawn to this group because we worked on experiments in spirituality, meaning we would discuss a lesson and then practice an action during the week that would be connected to the lesson. Actions were simple steps we could take in our lives, such as talking to someone we didn't know or giving an anonymous gift to a friend. Understanding a theory with the mind is one thing, but being able to harness the will to execute the desire proved to be quite challenging. It was a process of practical spirituality: learning to be thoughtful, kind and considerate to people in our environment. It also taught us to be mindful of our behavior and any discrepancy between our moral or spiritual code and our actions.

As I sat in the group one evening, I watched as each person shared and talked about their week and how they had incorporated the lessons. Without warning, a realization came. It was like a flash of lightning, revealing an insight that appeared suddenly in my conscious mind and disappeared just as quickly. I realized that I had been sitting with these same people for five years, but I did not feel a heart connection to any of them. We had discussed important values and practiced exercises in spiritual action, yet I knew nothing about who they were as people, such as whether they were married, whether they had children or any other personal facts. I felt no warmth toward them and had not even realized that I did not care enough to find out more. I asked myself how I could continue to do this when there was no heart involved. I knew the answer immediately and never returned. Like an old coat that was comfortable but too small, I had taken it off because it no longer served me.

I learned later that this was the beginning of the understanding that I could be easily seduced by intellectual pursuits. While they are noble in theory and we were at least trying to put kindness into action, it was all no more than academic process. I would learn that this seduction was, in reality, a common habit of the ego, which loves to pontificate and express itself through the intellect. Babaji would later teach me that if we are using the heart as our foundation, the rest comes easily, and we don't need exercises to practice our behavior.

How do I even begin to talk about the weeks leading up to my meeting with Babaji? How do I explain something for which there are no words? I have read that the ancient Egyptians had 50 different words for sand and the Eskimos have 100 different words for snow. Another culture has hundreds of words for the concept of love. How I wish I had thousands of words available for me to talk about Babaji.

Because of this paucity, I find myself taking the risk of relating the story of this time without being able to capture the true essence of the experience. To continue with my earlier metaphor of a hurricane, it was as if I were caught helplessly in a vortex of energy that shook me to my core and tossed me around like a wooden boat in a stormy sea.

It began benignly enough in the city of New Orleans, about a month after I left the ARE group. It was my first visit to Mardi Gras, and I was captivated by the energy and exuberance exhibited at the parades. As the floats passed by and the crowds surged around me to catch the flying beads that were thrown our way, I found myself gulping for breath. It was almost intolerable. Feeling a mixture of excitement, and now anxiety about my breathlessness, I was struggling to get enough air into my lungs. It was as if my body were a giant balloon that had been blown up to capacity and was now on the verge of popping.

Returning to Memphis, where I was living at the time, I embarked on a series of medical visits and allergy tests. It was finally pronounced that I was in excellent health, and I was told it must be psychosomatic. I made the decision to try and live with it and put it out of my mind.

While this was going on, my husband and I were in marital counseling. I think that my resentment about the roles I was trying to live out was finally getting the better of me, and we were both dissatisfied with our marriage the way it was. My husband was going through a midlife crisis and had purchased a bright red Fiero ,which was a poor man's sports car. I think his mortality was finally dawning on him and he was getting more and more difficult to live with.

Out of the blue, the counselor called to ask whether I was interested in getting my astrological chart done and making an appointment with an astrologer for him to read it. Knowing nothing about astrology, I declined the invitation. A week later, while folding laundry, I had a sudden urge to follow up to see if the astrologer had any openings. This was a spontaneous action that went against my previous decision. I made the appointment, and this was to become one of the biggest decisions of my life.

It's interesting to me that I am normally a slow, deliberate thinker and have a tendency to procrastinate and mull over decisions for a long time. In this case, I acted without mental reflection. It was as if my body knew what to do and impulsively acted. Looking back on my life, I realize that some of my biggest decisions were made from a deep bodily knowing that may have defied logic. The decision to marry my husband was made this way after only three months of knowing him. For me, this deep feeling comes from the stomach or the solar plexus. This is the third chakra of the body of energy medicine known as the chakra system. The third chakra is the center of personal power. It is also the hub of the nervous system. When I sense this knowing, it is as if there is an energetic click or connection that slides into place like a well-oiled lock. It is quite subtle but very convincing in its strength and clarity, which makes no sense at all to the logical and rational left brain.

I went to the appointment as scheduled the following week. As the astrologer talked at great length about quadrants and rising suns and moons, I wondered why I was there. I understood little of what he was telling me. He asked whether I had questions, and I didn't even know enough to ask him anything. He then dropped a bombshell when he said, "Before you go, I just want to tell you that you may be susceptible to breathing difficulties. Your chart shows no earth signs, which suggests this."

I was shocked and could not imagine how he would know about my breathing problems. *Has someone told him?* I asked myself. *How can he know this about me?* Suddenly, I was awake and alert. This may have been the first time I experienced synchronicity so powerfully, and this incident caused me to be mindful of more magical experiences hence forward. Jung described synchronicities as coincidences that have no causal foundation. It's when two entirely different aspects of our lives come together with no explanation. He described it as an archetypal process.

The astrologer then went on to say, "I can give you the name of someone who can help you with that." He wrote her name on a piece of paper and handed it to me. As I took it, a jolt of energy coursed through my body, and I felt as if I had been plugged into an electric power outlet. My body knew I had to meet this woman.

It took me over a week to finally set up an appointment with Christina Thomas Fraser, whose name had such a violent energetic and physical impact on me. I was impatient yet anxious, because I had no idea what to expect. I drove to her home and was ushered upstairs to a large, almost empty room. There was a small altar along one wall and backjacks on the floor. The pictures on the altar were foreign to me at the time, but somewhat comforting in their presence. I was to learn later that they were of Paramahansa Yogananda and His lineage. Yogananda was a great spiritual teacher who was the first to bring Eastern teachings to the West. He founded the Self Realization Fellowship in the United States and has been instrumental in introducing millions of people to an Eastern perspective of spiritual teachings and the nature of God, as well as an understanding of the relationship with God and guru as a personal one.

The expectations, excitement and fear were palpable for me as I sat quietly in this room, with no knowledge of the impact that the next few hours would have on me and my journey. It was to become a defining moment on my spiritual path and the cause of radical changes in my life.

Christina had told me she was a rebirther and could help me with my breathing problems. I had no idea what this meant, but I was willing to be open. I learned that rebirthing is a form of connected breathing that allows access to the unconscious and frequently produces life-changing experiences that result in a rebirth or a transformation. It was common for people to reexperience their birth during an episode of this breathing, which was instrumental in healing the birth trauma. Each experience is unique to the breather and enables them to understand more about their life and its challenges.

Today, this form of healing is quite well known and popular. In the early 1990s, there were only a few people offering this work. Breathwork was founded by Leonard Orr in the 60s. Sondra Ray started rebirthing around the same time and was known as the Mother of Rebirthing. She is a prolific author and workshop leader around the world. Both Leonard and Sondra were devotees of Haidakhan Babaji. Stanislav Grof came later. He was a psychiatrist whose work with Holotropic Breathwork helped legitimize this healing technique and move it into a mainstream acceptance.

Christina had me lie on the floor and taught me to breathe through the mouth, connecting the inhale to the exhale without stopping. She was sitting next to me on a backjack to support me and would occasionally breathe with me for a few breaths of encouragement.

The following is a description I wrote of what happened. Words are not adequate, so it seems that the fewer used, the better:

Struggle for breath
Struggle for Life
Parched mouth and a sense of choking
Living with little fluidity and retching on my own words
Will it never end?

"This is so hard," I tell myself
"I can't do it"
And the well-known mantra echoes in my ears

Pain and tightness in my body
Claw-like hands, almost intolerable
Why is there no help?
Continue to breathe the breath
With great difficulty
Suddenly
The breath is breathing me with
Powerful bellows
Now resting in the pre-dawn and post sleep
Place of recognition
I am relaxed,
Watching images drift before my eyes
No memory, no agenda

Suddenly clarity in a different realm
Where am I?
Does it even matter?
Transported on a strange and beautiful course
For which there are no words

A reunion of everything, known and unknown
Floating in an ocean of ecstatic bliss and peace
I am home and now I finally belong.
Peace, Joy and Contentment
At a level never known, yet always known
Bathed in echoes of ancient memories
Of perfect peace
A voice through the mists of my reverie
Is it God, my Higher Self?
An invitation to look at my body
My temple, my vehicle through life and human home
Overwhelmed with gratitude and at the same time
Filled with grief at my oft-times neglect and abuse of Her

"It's okay, she forgives you," said the voice
So much tenderness and kindness and perfect love as
I float into eternity

When I came back to earth, it was as if a different dimension had been added in my absence. Either that, or scales had fallen from my eyes. Everything was brighter and sharper, and I had to shield my eyes from the brilliance. I was left with a deep sense of peace and relaxation. About 20 minutes of disorientation were to follow as I asked myself, *What just happened to me?* I knew instinctively that my search had ended, and I had just discovered what I had been looking for since I was a young adult. This was the piece of the puzzle that had eluded me and prevented me from feeling happy. I finally felt complete and whole.

I had been picked up and set down firmly on my spiritual path, and my life would never be the same again. I had glimpsed Nirvana, and my old life had died away like the shedding of a snake's skin, as I was born into a different reality.

I finally felt grounded enough to drive home, and the world around me was magical. It had rained during the evening, and the streetlights magnified the raindrops that still glistened on the leaves and foliage and exaggerated their brilliant hues of varying shades of green. The road was twinkling from a carpet of sparkling diamonds. My senses were heightened, and I was acutely aware of the beauty of the evening. My mood was elevated. I had never felt this way before.

It was soon after this that I started to have dreams and visions of Babaji.

Notes

1 Irina Tweedie, *Daughter of Fire*, p. 84.

Personal Thoughts

Babaji appeared to me in a vision during meditation. I knew nothing about Him. His face was long and intense, and His gleaming eyes gave a penetrating look. His whole form was Divine to behold and His hair matched in exact detail a photo I held in my hand the next day. His mouth spoke silent words to me, yet He seemed to say: "Come Moy." Moy was my pet name when I was a child. . . .

I drove to a bookshop which was quite a distance away. I had to collect some pictures. While I was browsing through the books on display, the book Botschaft vom Himalaya fell into my hands. I opened it and caught sight of a picture. It was the same one as in my vision. I wasted no time in going to Babaji as I took it that He was calling me.[1]

—From *Babaji, the Unfathomable*,
edited by Gertraud Reichel

10.
VISIONS OF BABAJI

I am one of the fortunate people who discovered Babaji—or rather, He discovered me. There is a saying that the teacher, or guru, will appear when the student, or chela, is ready. This is an account of how He came into my life on that evening in 1991 when my life was immeasurably changed by Him.

After the rebirth experience with Christina, I was in a high energetic state that resulted in confusion and chaos in my inner life. My husband told me later that my body was vibrating so much that it was like sharing the bed with an electric dynamo. I would take a daily walk and had the desire to lie down on the sidewalk. It took all my strength not to submit to these weird impulses.

I went to a nine-day intensive with Christina and was completely out of control. The energy became so intense, all I could do was lie on the floor and surrender to powerful energy. It was like a Mack truck was being driven through my shaking body. Delving into spiritual teachings in the years to follow, I realized I was experiencing a kundalini awakening. *Kundalini* is a Sanskrit word that means "coiled" or "circular." Tantra teaches that it is a form of Divine feminine energy that sleeps like a serpent coiled up at the base of the spine. As the serpent begins to awaken, the energy flows upwards through the seven chakras (spiritual centers), and this leads to an expanded state of consciousness when it reaches the top. It can also be accompanied by unfamiliar feelings and impulses such as those described above. Not everybody experiences this phenomenon, so it can frequently be misdiagnosed and misunderstood.

One day, following another one of these powerful rebirthing episodes, I picked up a book that caught my eye as it lay on the coffee table. It was a large green book called *Babaji Mahavatar: The Descent of Eternity into Time*. I was particularly captivated as I gazed into Babaji's piercing eyes, which looked at me from the cover. As I glanced at the many-colored pictures of Him inside, I was transported to a different place and time. I was riveted by this Divine Being and the energy that emanated from every page. He was a combination of male and female, with shoulder-length curly dark hair or sometimes no hair at all. His sallow skin suggested an Eastern heritage, yet He could be European or pretty much any ethnicity. He could have been a man, or He could have been a woman. He was not of any gender or culture, but He embodied all genders and cultures. He was a paradox and an enigma, which made Him mesmerizing. It was as if He encompassed everyone, and even the entire world. It was His energy and His eyes, however, that were so captivating, as His energy poured through the pages of the book, quenching the thirst in my empty heart. I was drawn to Him like a moth to a flame.

I felt that I knew this Being and had known Him for eons of time, yet I wanted to find out more about Him. This is another example of the paradox I was caught in. As a fish struggling to gain release from a fishing net, I was desperately trying to see an exit from all the paradoxes surrounding me. Nothing made logical sense any more. My mind was virtually useless.

The dreams of Babaji started not long after this. Sadly, I was not in a state to think of writing these dreams down, and they came quickly and frequently. I remember seeing Him in my mind's eye. He had an Om sign on his forehead. I recognized the sign but did not know its meaning. I was to learn later that it is the highest sacred symbol in the Hindu religion. When it is sounded, it is said to produce powerful vibrations.

Slowly, His face would be replaced by my face—and the Om sign was now on me. I began to wake up from intense dreams about Him, and I would frequently smell the scent of roses, which would come out of nowhere and evaporate just as quickly as it came.

My waking and dreaming lives became as one, and I began to feel a loss of connection to reality as I knew it. He was so powerful that I questioned what was real, and at times, I questioned my own sanity. I had been raised in the Episcopal Church and believed in Christ, but I had never had such a powerful connection to Christ as I did to Babaji. In fact, I had never felt any personal connection to Christ at all.

It can be a very frightening time when one's world falls apart, together with all the precepts on which it has been built. There is a finality about it, a death of sorts, like the implosion of a derelict building by a demolition contractor. Explosives are used to destroy the building's main supports, causing it to collapse from the inside out. I was living through a human demolition, and Babaji was the contractor. The mold I had been born into was crushed into a million pieces by Him, and all I could do was wait for the rubble to settle before I could start to pick up the pieces and decide what I could salvage. Little did I know I had no choice in this, as I was already in Babaji's hands. He was now the sculptor of my life.

I was concerned about my dreams and visions, and I wondered whether I was descending into madness. I knew there was no one I could share my fears with, and that if I talked to a doctor, I would be hospitalized and labeled psychotic.

I had never felt more alone in the mortal world, and at the same time, it was as if I had an invisible guide. My sanity was saved by a deep, insistent knowing at the core of my being that I was okay and would rise from the ashes of my former life like a phoenix. I tried to understand this rationally and could come up with no answers.

I was to learn that Babaji was a Mahavatar, which means He was highly evolved and not born of a woman. He has the ability to materialize into a human form and dematerialize at will. In 1970, He was discovered as a young man, meditating in a cave in Haidakhan in the Himalayas in India. In this rural area where he was first encountered, He had never been seen before and the people knew nothing of his origins. He had come into the form of a young boy who appeared to be about 17 years old. In the 14 short years He was in His body, He became revered by thousands of people from all over the world, and without traveling far from the area in which He appeared. Physically, He aged many years during the short time He was on the Earth (see pictures at the center of the book).

It has been said that He took on the karma of many of His devotees so they could evolve faster. Under His leadership, an ashram was built near the cave where He appeared in Haidakhan. After His death in 1984, He has continued to attract people to His simple philosophy of truth, simplicity and love, the importance of service to the Divine and by His guidance as hundreds of people throughout the world continue to make pilgrimages to His ashram.

There is some difference of opinion about whether Babaji is the same Babaji mentioned in Yogananda's book, *Auto-biography of a Yogi*. Yogananda devoted an entire chapter to Babaji entitled "Babaji, Yogi-Christ of Modern India."[2] This Babaji was the guru of Lahiri Mahasaya, (guru of Yogananda's parents), and lived in the 19th century. He also lived in the

Himalayas and was a Mahavatar known as the deathless guru. He was described in much the same way as Haidakhan Babaji is described.

Many devotees I have spoken with say they found Babaji through *Autobiography of a Yogi*, and I heard that one devotee was in a bookstore when the book fell at her feet, leading her to search for Haidakhan Babaji.

When He came into my life, I knew none of this; in fact, I had never heard of Him. I just knew my spiritual thirst was continuing and the desire to quench it was becoming more demanding. At the same time, I was truly terrified that I was losing touch with reality. The result was that I was functioning in the world but inwardly adrift. The yardsticks I had in place by which to measure myself (previous beliefs, norms and values) were based on my early education—and suddenly, they were gone. I was living through something that nothing in my life could measure, understand or evaluate.

Looking back, I can say I had become addicted to this rebirthing process and my teacher in an attempt to recreate that first magical experience. I had slid into the trap of believing this was the answer to everything. I wanted to spend the rest of my life stringing these amazing episodes together. Boy, was I wrong! A new inner reality was being established, and I ultimately had to learn to live more fully in my body and the present moment.

Notes

[1] Gertrude Reichel, editor, Babaji-*The Unfathomable*: s.l. pp. 130-131.

[2] Paramahansa Yogananda, *Autobiography of a Yogi*, pp. 296-304.

We try to push all the parts of ourselves that we don't like into our bodies: our greed, our jealousy, our lust. All the darkness we don't want to accept, we push down into our muscles, bones and heart. We pretend we have no shadow and try to escape into our heads. Powerful energies are locked in our bodies. Eventually they rebel, usually in illness.[1]

—*Conscious Femininity*,
by Marion Woodman: Inner City Books

The path of God-realization is a most difficult one. Few are those who will walk it. It is as difficult as walking on the edge of a razor. The grace of the guru is everything. No knowledge is possible without the guru.[2]

—Babaji's words in *I Am Harmony*, by Radhe Shyam

To those who came for teaching and spiritual growth, Shri Babaji—the Supreme Guru—gave a rigorous training; one by one, He forced people to face and master the fears and desires that robbed them of courage and blocked out the Divine knowledge needed to walk the difficult path to Self-realization.[3]

—From *I Am Harmony*, by Radhe Shyam

11.
THE SHADOW REARS ITS UGLY HEAD

Having these visions of Babaji and meeting Christina brought me face to face with my shadow in a surprising and jolting way. At that time, I had no idea of the psychological concept of the shadow, but I was unknowingly in a collision with it. Thus began a lifelong dance with this enigmatic cloud that would follow me everywhere.

How do we know when something in our shadow has been triggered? It is often revealed when the intensity of emotion far outweighs the injustice of the indiscretion we perceive. This emotion, combined with instantaneous action or words, may result in asking ourselves afterwards, "What happened?" or, "Whatever came over me?" When we are acting from our shadow, our mind has gone into exile, so there is no thinking or rationale involved. It is as if a separate entity has entered our body and we are a puppet being pulled by its strings.

Christina was the catalyst for this first experience where I started to ask myself some of the above questions. After her, and for many years, my unconscious desire to find a mother resulted in my inwardly blaming others for abandoning me or failing to live up to my expectations. Intense and unconscious interactions with my shadow were indiscriminately scattering radioactive contents in my wake. One has to have courage and a strong love of adventure and enquiry in order to try and dance with the shadow in a meaningful way.

Robert Johnson, in his book *Owning Your Own Shadow*[4], describes it as the depository of all thoughts and ideas that go against our culture and our upbringing, and is the result of becoming civilized. If we are taught that it is wrong or sinful to think or act a certain way, these thoughts and actions go into an unconscious shadow bag. This is also true of the best and brightest parts of ourselves. If we have been raised and told that we will never amount to anything, all aspirations for a happy and successful life go into the shadow bag as well.

We live in a very narrow stranglehold of what is expected of us as a person. Part of the spiritual path requires that we explore our shadow and integrate it so that we move toward wholeness. The concept of individuation is not about achieving perfection but of achieving wholeness. We can only get to the light of who we are by passing through the shadow. Johnson says that owning our shadow means we have reached a sacred inner space that we cannot know any other way. Not working on our shadows means we fail to understand the Divine spark that we all carry.

I was learning about my shadow the hard way when these personal problems began to escalate with Christina. Our relationship became quite volatile as it turned into a carbon copy of the way I had interacted with my mother.

One day, as I was relaxing toward the end of a rebirthing session, I noticed her extend her hand with her palm down in deep concentration. My mother used to have the same mannerism as she admired her fingernails after she had given herself a manicure. She had pretty nails, and she was very proud of them. In contrast, I bit my nails for most of my childhood. She was constantly saying, "Don't you wish you had nails like mine?" as she made that same gesture. This resulted in my feeling even more worthless and inadequate than I normally did, and I felt my shortcomings were always being pointed out to me.

When Christina did this, it triggered all those early memories. Funny enough, a recent conversation with Christina revealed that she remembers noticing my nails with some admiration and wished she could have regular manicures! That's a good example of how we can misunderstand each other and live our lives based on our childhood experiences. I was seeing a negative that reinforced my beliefs, while in reality, I was receiving a compliment.

I felt confused and mortified by my negative thoughts and eruptions around her. I had managed to put my painful behavior behind me when I left England many years before, and now it was rearing its ugly head once more. I had projected my mother onto her and was acting as I had as a child. The situation became more complex, because I had given Christina the credit for my mystical experience. I think I believed she was able to bestow Divine experiences on everyone and this was her gift.

Like a child, I believed I could not live without her. I was endowing her with a power she didn't have, and I was furious when she didn't respond the way I expected her to. My dreams of Babaji were intrinsically connected to her, and I felt bound to her because of this. I loved her and hated her at the same time. I wanted more ecstatic moments and mistakenly thought they came as part of a package that only she could give me. She carried a magical quality for me that was totally unrealistic. To this day, I do not understand the dynamics that were playing out, but I do see it as the preliminary impetus for dealing with my shadow.

When baby ducklings are born, they imprint on the first thing they see. Usually, this is the mother duck, so everything works out well for them as they go to her for food and comfort and know to follow her and not get lost. If they see a human being, they accept this human as their mother and behave in the same way. I realized much later, when I entered therapy, that after I was reborn in the rebirthing experience, I had imprinted on Christina—and in that way, she had become a spiritual mother to me.

As our friendship became more complex due to the violent emotions I was experiencing, I became more confused. My feelings and thoughts were intense and irrational, as I realized I wanted to be around her more and more and felt abandoned and rejected when my desires were not met. I wanted to merge with her and became enraged when I realized she was her own person and separate from me. Was it the Divine energy I sensed in her that I wanted to merge with? Was it the infant part of me wanting to merge with mother?

Patricia Reis writes that there is a "painful longing" that has been set up in a woman "who has not had an affirming mother." She goes on to say, "This desire for fusion, in Freud's view, represented a regressive desire for the mother."[5] At this point in my life, that seems the most likely explanation for my bizarre feelings and desires.

Whatever was going on, from where I sit now, it was certainly a time of projecting my own shadow onto, and seeing my own inner gold, in another person. I knew I had to distance myself from Christina in order to find out who I was, and exactly who Babaji was.

Immediately following that life-changing episode, I felt like a highly evolved being from a different land and new to the mortal world. On the one hand, I felt more fully alive and whole than I had ever felt, but on the other hand, I had never felt more inept. I felt more alive because I was energized by the visions of Babaji. It was as if I were a 50-watt bulb that was plugged into a source (Babaji) that had raised my power to 100 watts. The ineptness came from the confusion and fear around my experiences. I was a child in a light body, and I wasn't sure how to function.

I felt I had lost my old self completely. Those yardsticks that had helped guide me had been swept away by an energetic tsunami, and I was left confused, vulnerable and upside down. Coping mechanisms I had used before were no longer working. These feelings continued for some time, and I found a Jungian analyst who was open and nonjudgmental and who helped me find some new ground in what felt like a groundless state.

Christina had recommended that I read two books, one being the Robert Johnson book about the shadow, and the other a book by Marion Woodman called *The Pregnant Virgin*. These books were instrumental in helping to pave the way to a new sanity and creating a foundation for my future. I would function nearly normal in the daytime, and then I would return home and read them every evening. They are both full of yellow marker underlining and were an important part of my journey.

Owning Your Own Shadow helped me see my journey in a more positive light and gave me the confidence to begin to take responsibility for my happiness, and ultimately, my future. Marion's book was about inner transformation for women, and it became a mirror to me as I saw myself reflected in the words she had written. I remember asking myself: *How can this woman possibly know what I have been thinking and feeling for most of my life?*

Both books were also instrumental in the changes in my outer world as I went into Jungian psychoanalysis and returned to university to study psychology. Unbeknownst to me, it was also preparation for future work with Marion Woodman.

What were the long-term effects of this numinous experience? Now, almost three decades later, I am still trying to understand them. How would I have been any different had none of this happened to me? All I know is that it did happen, and I can share some of my reflections on the differences it has made in my life.

I think until that point, even though I felt something within me was missing, I was taking life at face value and not realizing the depth of myself and the potential for personal growth that lay there. I was unaware that there was an inner path and was putting most of my energy into living in the "real world." Of course, what I thought of as the real world was the world of illusion. I came to understand that my inner world was the only real world, as it held my own personal truths. This realization had the effect of launching me on an inner journey.

Integrating shadow qualities was crucial to the start of this journey because I was only glimpsing a fraction of the picture of who I was. It was like seeing a large iceberg floating benignly on the surface of the water and never knowing the size and depth of what lay beneath or recognizing the full form and texture of this magnificent structure.

The psychological and spiritual journey will carry you on an underwater tour of the iceberg, which will take the rest of your life to explore and you will never fully complete. As the ice melts and re-freezes with different temperatures, so we resist and surrender through the varying conditions that come into our lives. Our inner form undergoes subtle changes in the process. If we are in tune with this miraculous unfolding, it makes our lives richer and more meaningful.

At that time, I began in earnest to try and make sense of what had happened to me and continued to do this for many years. I would search for answers and an explanation but realized there were none that fit into my prior concept of the world and life itself. Jungian beliefs and writings helped me to eventually accept this, because they presented me with a larger framework that held both spiritual and psychological truths. I was able to broaden my understanding of both.

I have since learned that there are many things that happen in our lives we cannot make sense of. These may include birth and death, catastrophic accidents, illnesses and environmental disasters. "What caused them? How did they happen? Could I have done anything different to avoid them?" we ask ourselves, and then we can spend years focusing on these questions and receiving no answers. These situations are usually outside of our control, and they hopefully prompt us to eventually accept that there is a force greater than us that has the ultimate power. They test our resolve and willingness to surrender. Over time, they deepen our spiritual faith and our trust in ourselves. There's a huge caveat here, however. Surrender is an important part of the process. We can either surrender to our destiny and attempt to work with it, or we can resist and become bitter and angry. This is part of the spiritual and psychological work of becoming more conscious. Frequently, our biggest gifts are found in our most challenging times that defy understanding. We may not realize it at the time, but we can see it more clearly when we look back.

That time in my life reveals to me just how important it is for us to be aware of the mold we have been born into and the effects of our childhood conditioning. If we never understand this, we will never be free to assess the stories we tell ourselves and to change them. These tales will then remain in the unconscious, where they continue to influence our lives—often in a negative way.

Immediately following this incident, new teachers and mentors began to appear, and I looked for ways to make life more meaningful. I also changed careers and became more focused and self-directed. I became passionately committed to working with people and living a life of service. I had never enjoyed the computer profession I had entered at my father's suggestion, although I had found it interesting. Now I knew that I wanted to work with people, and I wanted to help those who were struggling with emotional problems. I realize now that I was moving from a more patriarchal stance to one that was more feminine, involving compassion and understanding.

I recently heard a Jungian analyst say that it is a numinous experience that sets us on the spiritual path. The psychological path focuses on the mind and our beliefs, and provides tools for dealing with the outside world. These may be tips for dealing with anxiety or depression, or communication problems with a partner. The psychological path becomes a spiritual path only after a numinous experience because, as Lionel Corbett explains in the book, *Jung and Aging*, we then feel supported by a Divine presence that is larger than ourselves.[6] My experience with Babaji caused me to have personal knowledge of a Divine force or power, which is vastly different from just having a certain theoretical perspective or belief.

When I look back, this was the moment my life took a completely different direction. I was reborn into a world that was centered in the heart, which I had unknowingly asked for when I left the ARE study group. As a newborn baby must learn to live in the world and accomplish challenging feats like learning to talk and walk, I had to learn how to adjust to this new world into which Babaji had delivered me.

I believe we can have many symbolic births during our lifetime, and we don't have to physically die to be reborn. This period was easily the most agonizing and horrendous time of my life. I felt as if I had been held and dropped from a great height, landing in a place that was unknown and frightening. The ground I thought I had been standing on was no longer there. I went through episodes of extremes of emotions; I could be jubilant one minute and very depressed the next. I had to work on leveling out my emotions.

The most challenging aspect for me was withdrawing all the projections I had placed on Christina. It took many years to do this successfully. I was helped by Robert Johnson's book, my analysis and my entry into the local Jung seminar program. I had to learn the meaning of projection, which involves seeing the parts of ourselves, both good and bad, mirrored in another person. I then had to try to understand what exactly I was projecting onto her. It took a few years to forgive myself and Christina for any distorted views I had of her, as well as perceived hurts and insults I had buried. The details of these offenses are not important; it is the fact that we are willing to let them go and move on, and more importantly, to be able to search into our shadow to understand our own contribution to these difficult situations.

It is clear to me now that I was projecting a perfect mother (the mother I never had) onto Christina, who could never have lived up to such expectations. I had to forgive myself for expecting her to be perfect and to be there for me in ways my mother could not be. I had to forgive myself for projecting my inner gold onto her because I was unable to see it in myself. In doing this, over time I was able to learn to mother myself, see Christina as a human being and claim those golden aspects of her that also belonged to me.

I utilized a forgiveness process that took almost a year to complete, since my anger and resentment kept getting in the way. Forgiveness is a word that is frequently heard and easily tossed about between people, as if in the tossing, the act has been completed. My experience has been that forgiveness is one of the most important and difficult actions we can take. The word may roll off the tongue easily, but the action must sometimes be pried out of the heart.

You must reach deep into your heart and tell yourself continually that you are doing this process for yourself and yourself alone. Forgiving people does not condone their actions or make everything right; it releases *you* from the grip of toxic feelings. Whatever the other person has done or failed to do is directed by your personal story about them, so in fact, may not be based in reality at all. Also, their behavior is theirs to resolve with their God and has nothing to do with you. In my case, my feelings were so strong that it took me a year to be able to complete a forgiveness process that could have been finished in seven days.

It is also crucial that we take the time to forgive ourselves for past actions and thoughts. Sometimes, these have been buried so deeply that we need professional help to uncover them. If we don't accomplish this, we will be battling with unfinished, unconscious business until we die, and maybe even after death.

It was to take more years before I could complete the withdrawal process and finally reconcile with the person who had opened the door for me to fully embark on my spiritual and psychological path. This began with tentative phone calls between us. We never mentioned anything that had happened and kept our conversations limited to what was going on in the present. Over time, we developed a valued and abiding friendship.

Today, I have the deepest love and respect for Christina. Two years ago, I spent a long weekend with her and her family in California. Now, when I think back to those tumultuous days, it is with deep gratitude that defies normal human feelings, for she is my spiritual mother who birthed me into a new consciousness that changed the entire course of my life.

The journey through the shadow toward the light is frequently called the dark night of the soul, a term coined by the Christian saint John of the Cross. It is a time of deep introspection and inner pain. This does not normally take place in isolation. We are still expected to attend to the daily aspects of living and fulfilling our roles as wives, breadwinners, mothers etc. It's a challenging time as we try to function as usual in the outside world while our inner world is in a state of flux and our emotions are screaming at us.

The dark night of the soul is an underground path that is foreign and frightening. It requires spending a long period of time in the dark, never really knowing if you will see the light of day again. For me, it happened suddenly and unexpectedly and was initiated by a numinous experience. I am sure it can happen in many ways: maybe a slow but persistent idea that you may have something to do with a scattering of failed relationships in your wake, or at a time when you are feeling very good about yourself and your life because you are meditating daily and teaching yoga. What I do know is that it is unstoppable; once it has its eyes on you, there is no way to avoid it and no way around it. The only way to get over it is to move through it, one day at a time.

Entering this space was a period of ultimate aloneness, for how could I even verbalize that period of absolute darkness and horror? It was also a time of deep questioning. Everything I had ever believed or known was falling away, and I was being called to develop new concepts. It was the clashing of two worlds, the Divine and the Mortal.

Our culture is not set up to easily recognize this rite of passage, and it can be mistakenly diagnosed, or worse still, end in hospitalization. It is crucial to find someone who under-stands this initiation and can support you. I use the words *rite of passage* and *initiation* because that is really what this part of the spiritual path is. It is provided by Grace and an invitation to enter the shadow or belly of who we are. It ultimately expands our horizons and helps us redefine our lives in a way that provides deep meaning. It is a beckoning from the light of the Divine.

It is not surprising that this period frequently shows up in midlife. I was in my early forties. It is at this time, when the ego becomes strong enough to break, that the dark night looms on the horizon. It teaches us to depend on something other than the ego—and that is almost always something unseen that cannot be found in the outside world. It calls for faith in that which is larger than us, and it also calls for patience and tenacity. These are all important values for our spiritual journey.

My experience with Babaji and the accompanying visions upset the apple cart in terms of the way I had previously understood life and the world around me. I felt the seismic shift in the ground beneath me, but I didn't understand it or know what it was. I was tempted to seek psychiatric help and instead went on a search to really understand who this person was who had so profoundly shaken my sense of reality.

I knew at some deep level that I was where I was meant to be, and I learned to trust the knowing which was always present like a magnet nudging me forward gently with reassurance. It taught me to trust this inner guidance rather than the views of the collective and the established medical community. It was a very scary and lonely time.

Added to these inner challenges, people who are experiencing a dark night of the soul are also called to deal with the outside world and friends and family members who see that all is not right with us. They express concern and give advice when they have no idea of the turmoil we are inwardly carrying. We must often hold down jobs and don't have the luxury of shutting ourselves away so we can tend to this unstable inner event.

During this time, I set up an altar and claimed a room in the house as my private and personal space. I would pray to Babaji daily and spend time in meditation. This was the beginning of my daily spiritual practice. I was also reading books about Him and the experiences of other people who had been impacted by Him in a similar way. These stories written by others helped validate my own. He was the magnet described above, and like a beacon in the darkness, He prevented me from losing my way completely. He was a continuous presence inside as I strove to deal with the outside changes of returning to school and entering analysis. I began to think more about my childhood, and I began to question and try to understand who I was and what I really wanted. By doing this, I was also beginning to take responsibility for myself and my actions. I had never even thought about these things before.

It is extremely difficult to adequately describe my state during this time, because the only words that come close are *precarious* and *chaotic*. How does one talk about chaos? My life was changing at a rapid speed, and I no longer recognized it. It was as if it belonged to someone else, and maybe it did, for Babaji was definitely in control.

I intuitively knew that it was important for me to stay grounded in my own new, emerging reality. I did this by volunteering at a local riding school to clean out the stalls every weekend in return for riding lessons. I used to look forward to these early morning weekends when I was alone with the horses and shoveling poop! The horses had a calming presence for me, and I loved the smells, which helped me feel closer to the Earth. By the time I had finished my chores, I was exhausted, but it was a healthy, grounded exhaustion to which I could relate. I also walked often and spent time outside.

At that time, surprisingly for me, I seemed to have more clarity about my immediate direction and priorities. There was no question in my mind that I would stop searching for more understanding about Babaji. I knew He was my guru, and I would follow Him until death and beyond. I even accepted the fact that He was more important to me than my earthly relationships and I would even be willing to sacrifice my marriage for Him if it were required. I fervently hoped that this would not be the case and that my husband would be able to find a way to accept the new person I was becoming. I understood at a very deep level that our relationship could not survive and flourish if there was no God present, and to me, Babaji was God in a form to whom I could relate.

I kept thinking about how Christ called Peter the disciple in the New Testament. He went down to the Sea of Galilee and told him to put down his nets and follow Him. Peter immediately did as he was asked. I felt the same way about Babaji. He was already so important to me, I knew I would follow Him anywhere.

I now understand that after the demolition Babaji had initiated, He was burning away all the delusions I had been living under and teaching me a new vision. I was now burning in the Fire of Love.

Notes

[1] Marion Woodman, *Conscious Femininity*, p. 137.

[2] Radhe Shyam, *I am Harmony*, p. 201.

[3] Ibid., p. 204.

[4] Robert Johnson, *Owning Your Own Shadow*.

[5] Patricia Reis, *Daughters of Saturn*, p. 129. Used with permission of the author.

[6] Leslie Sawin, Lionel Corbett and Michael Carbine, editors, *Jung and Aging*, p. 223.

Personal Thoughts

Granny (great grandmother), circa 1950's

Nan and grandad, circa 1960

Me with Santa Claus, circa 1949   Me with doll, circa 1950

Me with mum and dad—1969

Tom and me on our wedding day—1974

Me and Tommy, circa 1974

Tommy with friend Pete,
circa 1979

Temple side of the river at Indian Ashram

Crestone Ashram temple.

Divine Mother Murti in temple

Sacred Fire in India

Sharda and Ramloti
in FL, circa 2015

Me in India.

(L to R) Ramloti, friend Olga,
Me, friend Sarena

Babaji, circa 1974

Babaji, circa 1982

You can kiss your family and friends good-bye and put miles between you, but at the same time you carry them with you in your heart, your mind, your stomach, because you do not just live in a world but a world lives in you.[1]

—Frederick Buechner

12.
THE JUNGIAN WAY

We are not meant to lead isolated lives, so our connections with people, whether fleeting or long-term and regardless of depth, are instrumental in our own personal healing and happiness. We are creating a play called *Life* that consists of many different actors and actresses. We are the producers of this drama, and its purpose is to help with our spiritual healing on our way back home to Source or God.

Given that, it is crucial to recognize the most important relationship we will ever develop is the one with ourselves. Jungian psychology refers to individuation, which is the process of becoming more of who we really are as we integrate different aspects of ourselves, particularly the shadow. This is a lifelong process, and at an unconscious level, we create many different characters and situations that allow us to do just that.

Teachers and guides have been an integral part of my life, and I could not have progressed without them. For me, they have been psychotherapists, authors, friends and neighbors. Every relationship we have contains the nucleus for healing.

This book is about my journey with Babaji, but everybody we encounter is a guru to us, in that they reflect back parts of ourselves we like or hate, or sometimes both. I frequently have to ask myself, "What is the lesson this person is giving me?" when I face challenging relationship issues. The most impactful lesson I have learned is to walk away when relationships have been toxic.

None of us have a roadmap for life; we just adopt the map used by our parents and generations before us, and we are expected to muddle through and cope with everything that comes along, believing it to be our fate. It is too bad that there is still such a stigma around seeing a counselor or psychologist, who can help us to ask ourselves important questions that lead to our healing and individuation. Our quick-fix culture has many believing that we can medicate away depression and anxiety, when in fact, they are the voices of the body's wisdom that are desperately trying to tell us something is wrong.

It was an enormous boon to me that I discovered Marion Woodman and Robert Johnson and subsequently entered therapy. They both became important teachers and guides for me.

The Jungian analysis I embarked upon was a time of deep learning. Jungian analysts and Jungian-oriented therapists are focused on understanding the unconscious. This means the personal unconscious, as well as the collective unconscious. A therapist who works from this perspective helps us uncover beliefs we are not aware of and that do not serve us as adults. In fact, Jung famously stated that what we do not make conscious comes to us as fate. This means that life is not happening to us as a result of fate, but rather, as a result of sabotaging beliefs in the unconscious.

The good news is that they can be changed. Many of these beliefs arise in our childhood because of our environment, and they severely obstruct any hope of achieving our unique potential. Examples of these may be, "I am not good enough", "People do not listen to me", "I was a mistake", etc. The results of these untruths with which we live can be revealed in our dreams and in continued conversation with a therapist who is able to see into our blind spots. Myths and fairy tales act as guides by relating the human condition in a form of simple storytelling.

Most Jungian therapists see our journey through the lens of spirituality and understand the center of the psyche to be the Self, or the Divine essence of who we are. They understand life to be a mystery, a search for meaning and a journey to this innermost treasure. It was this philosophy that drew me into the Jungian world as I strove to understand the meaning behind my spiritual experiences and my life with Babaji.

Jung had an inner guide he called Philemon. He talks about him in his book, *Memories, Dreams and Reflections*. He saw Philemon as a fantasy character with whom he conversed and received teachings. It did not dawn on him that Philemon could have been a guide who inhabited another dimension. One day Jung was visited by a friend of Gandhi's, and Jung was brave enough to ask him about the nature of his guru. He was astounded when the Indian told him his guru was Shankaracharya, who was a teacher of the Vedas many centuries before. The Indian went on to say, "There are ghostly gurus, too . . . most people have living gurus. But there are always some who have a spirit for a teacher."[2]

This was very validating for Jung, who only then began to understand that perhaps Philemon was a spirit teacher and not a mere fantasy of his unconscious. Reading this was enormously validating for me, because it helped corroborate my sense of Babaji and how I saw Him in my world.

In contrast to Jungian analysis, regular therapy or counseling is different in that it focuses on solving current problems in the outside world, such as relationship issues, work problems, depression or anxiety. Therapy is more goal-directed, and there is usually a treatment plan over the course of the treatment. Anxiety and depression are treated with medication, and relaxation skills are taught to clients to help alleviate these symptoms. These modalities do not consider the unconscious, the effect of our formative years or dreams.

I have learned in my role as a dream counselor that if a client brings a dream when (s)he first comes to therapy, the dream will tell us why (s)he is there. It is the springboard from which we work. If there is no dream, we flounder for a while, with no sense of direction. People are usually in therapy for a deeper reason than they think they are. The dream will reveal this. We can then focus on the core truth for that person and not the story they are telling themselves.

Pulling up a weed by its roots causes it to be gone for good, while lopping off leaves or cutting the weed back just causes greater growth. Clients usually present with symptoms, and if they alone are treated, the problem will never be reconciled and more symptoms will arise in their place.

I have learned this from experience, but back then, as a member of a local Jung group, I was attending monthly meetings and periodic dream workshops. I had just walked through a portal into a new world of dreams and fairy tales, myths and legends. I found exploration of the unconscious through dreams fascinating and quickly understood their relevance to understanding ourselves and our lives.

The greatest gift to me was learning to fully understand symbolism and how it speaks to us. My first big dream, which resulted in my moving to Canada, revealed that I had basic, raw understanding of symbols, but my Jungian path deepened and refined this knowledge. This was an ongoing process that flowered during my work with Marion, which was to come later.

Our dreams are full of symbols, meaning they represent something other than what they are. For example, dreams of death do not usually foretell an actual physical death but suggest a symbolic death or the end of something. A dream allows us to ask ourselves, "What is it within me that is going to die in order for something new to be born?"

We may dream of a starving animal that is locked away in a shed. We are being asked what we associate with that particular animal and how we might be abusing that aspect of ourselves. These symbols carry enormous energy. Some of our dream images can stay in our minds for weeks or months, and some even for a lifetime.

Marion Woodman describes them as transformers that hold intense energy and are capable of healing psyche and body. Symbols work on the emotions, the mind and the imagination, so they are part matter and part spirit. These images arise in the subtle body or energy body, which is found where the physical meets the spiritual in a place I call *soul*. I see soul as our own unique and individual spiritual Self that matures with age. The language of soul is metaphoric or symbolic.

I was attracted to this new Jungian world because it represented to me an intermediary space that existed between the spirit realm, with which I was familiar, and the mortal world. I grew to love and respect this rich symbolism that was now revealing itself to me, and I quickly determined that I wanted to pursue the path of psychological and emotional understanding as a career.

This dovetailed with Babaji's teachings about the importance of karma yoga, or work as service. In the book *I Am Harmony*, it is said that Babaji described karma yoga as "the most important act of religion" and noted that in this age we can "reach liberation only through hard work." He said that work is our duty and we must perform it mindfully, in harmony with creation and by offering our actions to God. He also said it should not be done for selfish reasons or "motivated by hatred, jealousy, greed, lust, revenge."[3]

I couldn't imagine anything I would rather do than commit myself to a future of listening to and witnessing the lives of those who wanted to know more about themselves. I would do this to the best of my ability and offer the results to God.

Today, I am reminded of this frequently when I sit with clients and wonder why they continue to return when they don't seem to be benefitting from our work together. Immediately, when I have this thought, I remind myself that I cannot be the judge of that—and once more, I offer these services to Babaji.

I decided to return to school and work toward completing my undergraduate degree and then my master's degree in social work. My plan was to become a psychotherapist with a Jungian orientation. The details fell into place easily and I knew that this was my calling, as the doors were being opened for me.

While my inner world was rich and meaningful, my relationships were crumbling around me and I was scared and lonely. My husband was not happy about the changes I was making and the resulting effects on his life. He told me he could not support me to go back to school. This was like waving a red flag to a bull for me, and I quickly advised him that I could support myself and this was something I had to do.

We agreed to a trial separation, and I went to live in a granny flat belonging to a friend who lived near the university. I applied for college grants. I was angry with my husband and very scared that our marriage would not be able to survive this.

Patricia Reis talks about this phenomenon in *Daughters of Saturn*, saying that women, if they are to find their own autonomy, have to cross over "the threshold," which signals a separation from everything we have ever known in a male-dominated society. She writes, "This step is not done without trepidation. And, if the woman is heterosexual, one of the most compelling fears, one of the hardest risks she faces is loss of communication with, approval by, and love from the man (or the men) in her life."[4]

Not realizing it at the time, I was standing on the threshold of a new life, but I knew my biggest fear was losing my husband.

It is surprising to me that I cannot remember in detail the personal torment that I went through as I faced the possibility of losing Tom. I was dealing with a mixture of emotions. I felt in my bones that the steps I was taking were right for me...but would they be accepted and supported by the man I loved? I had no answers.

Our marriage survived two separations, each one lasting a year. As I look back, I am not even sure when they occurred, but I do know this was the second and final separation we went through. The first was his decision as he attempted to negotiate a midlife crisis, and the second was my decision. After both reconciliations, our relationship was stronger and healthier. After the second one, I learned that when he said he would not support me, he meant that we were not financially in a position to pay college fees and give up one income. Sadly, our communication was so poor that he was unable to express this clearly, and I was so rebellious that I just heard the words, "I can't support you," and thought he meant emotionally, after which point I took the situation into my own hands.

I was carrying the belief that I had to do everything alone, and there was no point in asking for or expecting support. It was during the reconciliation after the second separation that I finally told him I objected to the role I had fallen into. I told him that I didn't want to feel pressured to have a meal ready every night, and I objected to the expectation that I would clean and wash laundry every week. His humorous response was, "I thought you did those things because you liked to do them. It doesn't matter to me."

Our marriage resumed, and he learned to cook and operate the washer and dryer! For the first time in our marriage, I felt free to be myself and felt better understood as a person. Our marriage was now a partnership, and I relished in this. For his part, he stopped trying to care for me in a way that felt suffocating at times. When I had a problem, he would listen and not try to fix it for me. He treated me with greater respect and concern. I think it was at that point we started to deepen our love and mindfully demonstrated this by our actions toward each other.

Each time we reconciled, I saw Tom differently. I used to be in awe about how much he had changed, and then in confusion I would think, *Has he changed, or have I changed?* There was no easy answer to that, and maybe we both had.

I believe it was a time of us both pulling back the projections we had on each other. We were seeing each other realistically for the first time, in all our strengths and all our weaknesses, and deciding whether we liked each other enough to continue. Love as a feeling was evolving into love as an action and a commitment.

Marion Woodman talks about this moment of clarity in relationships when she talks of her own marriage and the first time she saw her husband without a projection:

We had been married 25 years. It was early morning. I had awakened cranky and discontent. I was sitting in the living room drinking my coffee, thankful for the silence. Then he decided to get up and make his own breakfast. I saw him in the kitchen trying to break an egg into a single little egg poacher. He was in his old

Black Watch housecoat, his two spindly legs sticking out the bottom. "I deserved better than this," I thought. But as I watched him patiently cutting his bread, there was something about the concentration of his hand on the loaf that caught a lifetime in a moment. "He's still here," I thought. "I'm still here. We're in this little box on the seventeenth floor in a place called Toronto with a crazy world out there. Whatever life is, we've walked our parallel paths together. God knows, I've made him suffer, and he's made me suffer. But we're here. Neither of us has given up the search." I respected him. Whatever the mystery is that holds two people together exploded through my heart. Aware of my old housecoat and not so thin legs, I knew that human love and Divine love are the same essence.[5]

I read this paragraph more than 25 years ago, and it caused a spark of joy in my heart and made me laugh out loud with a feeling of relief. Who could not love this woman and her audacity to speak such truths? I loved that she had the courage to put into words phrases that I was now recalling had lived on the periphery of my awareness. What woman after 25 years of marriage had not said to herself, "I deserve better than this!"? I know I had. I also knew I had those moments with Tom when I was entranced by something he did or said, or just an expression on his face that endeared me to him and caused the exploding heart reaction that Marion talks about. I, too, could relate to the suffering we caused each other. What is the glue that binds two people together on a common journey? It is the grace of God, and as Marion says, part of the mystery of life.

I know that our final separation caused me to realize that Tom was my best friend, and I didn't want to lose him. I loved and respected his loyalty and his recent ability to swallow his ego and find a new way that worked for both of us. He was always there for me, even when it seemed he wasn't. I could feel the depth of his love, and my heart was resonating with his.

All was not well with my parents at this time. They were not happy with me and expressed to Tom they were scared I was being indoctrinated into a cult. They never spoke to me about this, so it was easy to avoid talking to them about the things that mattered most to me. I continued to dutifully visit with them every week, and we sat together making small talk and making few, if any, nicks into the veneer of our relationship.

There was one very therapeutic period while I was undergoing analysis, when I decided to return to South Wales with my mum to help her explore her roots. She wanted to write about her time in the orphanage as a child and asked me if I would go with her to try and track down old schoolfriends and see where the orphanage was located. It was a trip down memory lane for her, and since she rarely undertook anything that might affect her emotionally, I wanted to share it with her. It was a special time for both of us and became a bonding experience that I truly valued.

The orphanage was in a small fishing village near Swansea in South Wales. It was picturesque, with hills that rose abruptly from the sea and that could be accessed by narrow lanes that were flanked with colorful small cottages. Mum took us to the spot where the orphanage used to be. It was no longer there, but she was able to track down an elderly woman whom she remembered going to school with. Mum reminisced at length with this woman and with me. She had never been as open before, and I caught glimpses of who she really was underneath the fun-loving bravado that she presented to the world and without the anger I saw as a child. I learned that it was her job as a child to take the orphanage's baked goods to houses in the village to sell them. She spoke with great passion about her walks over the hills and the people who befriended her. She loved Lady, the nun who ran the home and she would do anything for her. I realized for the first time that she had some happiness here, for it was all she had ever known. It was only when she was taken away by her father that her misery set in. This was exacerbated by a growing understanding of what she had missed by not having loving parents to raise her.

This trip brought us closer together and was a healing time for both of us. She said things to me that she had never uttered before—about how she always felt unloved and had to go above and beyond in her relationships to get people to love her. She shared that she had cultivated a special place in Lady's heart, and it gave her satisfaction to know that she was her favorite child. As she talked, I resonated with her words and was struck by the fact that it could be me talking about my feelings. I realized I had absorbed and carried a lot of her beliefs, and I could see how so much pain gets passed from one generation to another.

It was good that I was in therapy at this time. I had the time and space to sort through all of this and consciously return to Mum all the beliefs I was carrying that came from her and that no longer worked for me. It was a time of letting go and discovering who I was as separate from her.

Unknown to me at the time, this period of intense emotion and upheaval was actually a time of healing and reconciliation. I could only see this in retrospect, because while I was going through it, my attention was focused only on the chaos and insecurity. Like calm waters miles below a rough surf, I had no idea that Babaji was at work, healing my relationships and helping me to establish a profession moving forward.

This taught me that not everything is at it seems, and the greatest gifts come from some of the most difficult times. Little did I know I could trust the calm waters beneath the everyday turmoil. Relationships were being mended, and doors were being opened for me that would impact the rest of my life. My introduction to Carl Jung's work was to be hugely significant.

After Babaji demolished the mold into which I was born, He was slowly and carefully constructing a new one during this intense period of rebuilding. He had reduced me to a lump of clay and was busy gouging and chiseling according to His unique vision for me and my life.

Notes

[1] Frederick Boechner, *Telling the Truth: The Gospel as Tragedy, Comedy and Fairy Tale*, p. 3.

[2] CG Jung, *Memories, Dreams and Reflections*, pp. 183-184.

[3] Radhe Shyam, *I am Harmony—A book about Babaji*, pp. 245-246.

[4] Patricia Reis, *Daughters of Saturn*, p. 183. Used with permission of the author.

[5] Marion Woodman, *The Ravaged Bridegroom—Masculinity in Women*, Inner City Books, p. 211.

Personal Thoughts

Thou art the moonlight Mother. Thou alone
Shineth
in the pure light of the blazing sun.
The radiance of the stars is Thy reflection.
Thou art the burning ardour of the fire,
in water, soft fluidity Thou art.
Thou art the Earth, upholding all Creation,
Unrivalled is Thy Power's splendour
As Vishnu's Shakti Thou upholdeth and blesseth the world.[1]

No-one can even dream to count
the jewels at the bottom of the ocean.
And even a gifted poet can't describe
The brilliant splendour of the sun.
In this way, Bliss-bestowing Mother of the Universe
Who in this world is able
to tell the tale of Thy Magnificence and Glory ?[2]

—Haidakhandi Sapta Sati, by Shastriji. pp 182 and 228

13.
FINDING MY SPIRITUAL HOME AND FAMILY

I am reminded again of Clarissa Pinkola Estes' retelling of "The Ugly Duckling." It takes the duckling many adventures and much heartache before he finally finds his family of swans. This comes with the realization that he really is one of them and was accidentally born into a family of ducks. Estes says this fairy tale has two main meanings. The first is that the duckling symbolizes our wild nature and the ability to be persistent and never give up. The second important message of the story is that when someone is recognized and validated at a soul level, it makes them feel more alive and more powerful.[3]

I had not yet discovered my spiritual family, and although I was not aware of it, I was now closer to finding it. I was still carrying this longing, which I have described as a Divine longing. As a human being, I desperately wanted to feel as if I belonged. I was not willing to sacrifice myself to achieve this sense of belonging and acceptance, so I carried a constant ache and conflict. I think this is what my father had referred to when he said, "You will never find what you are looking for."

Besides looking for belonging, I was also looking for my tribe: people who could understand me and who were coming from a similar standing. This would be a place where I would feel at home and accepted for who I was.

My destiny was taking me on two separate paths: my spiritual path with Babaji and my psychological path with Jung.

It felt as if I were walking both paths at the same time. I was traversing the road to psychological individuation at the same time as I was on the road to cosmic oneness. This sounds like a contradiction, but I was to learn that I had to know and love myself before I could approach anything close to oneness. My rebirthing experience had given me a taste of it, but there was more to come.

In my psyche, I could not reconcile this paradox back then. I kept both roads separate from each other, and I shared the Babaji path with very few people who were not in the immediate Babaji community. I had learned as a child to keep everything hidden that was close to my heart. I went to great lengths to keep my spirit world and my Babaji experiences a secret. I feared being ridiculed and made to feel more of an outsider than I already felt. I don't think I even shared these self-forbidden episodes with my analyst.

Only recently have I realized that these seemingly distinct paths were one and the same. Writing this book and speaking with an analyst again has helped me understand this. Back then, I knew I had to find a way to gain more clarity about this Babaji being who continued to show up in my dreams. Was He in some way connected only to Christina? Was I able to perceive Him only because of her? I had so many questions and no answers that satisfied me.

One day, I learned that another Babaji devotee named Shdema Goodman was having a weekend workshop at her home in New Jersey. She had written a book called *Babaji, Meeting with Truth*, and she had been fortunate enough to be with Babaji when He was in His body. I had devoured this book and had readily identified with her when she talked about her rebellion and the fact that Babaji threw her out of the ashram numerous times.

Shdema explained that Babaji knew everyone's weaknesses. It was as if He could see inside them. He would trigger her vulnerabilities, causing her to think about what He was trying to teach her. Still, she did not give up and would sleep outside the gates or go to a local town. She would finally be allowed to enter when her thinking changed, and she would understand why she had been asked to leave.

One time, He shouted at her to "Go!" and she had no idea why. He told her to leave and go to her American friend. She relates that this action caused her to relive a lifetime of pain around rejection. She searched for the only American she knew, and after hearing her story, he told her, "Of course, that is why He threw you out. You were giving Him so much power. You give everybody power'."

She said at that point that she was able to see how she ingratiated herself to people in order to feel acceptance and love. Babaji was teaching her to be herself and to love herself unconditionally. After much soul-searching and with great trepidation, she finally had the courage to return, and He eventually let her come back into the ashram.4

From reading Shdema's book, I learned more about Babaji. He had been in His body from 1970 to 1984, and many in the Babaji community had been with Him in India during this time. This information confirmed to me that I was not going "crazy," and the Babaji who was appearing to me in visions and dreams was an actual person who had lived during my lifetime. This meant there were people who had been with Him and could tell me more about Him. Shdema was one of these people. This was further confirmation and validation for me of the existence of a world of spirit.

I set off on a pilgrimage to New Jersey to hopefully learn more about this fascinating guru. The weekend was helpful to me, as I realized that Babaji could speak through many different people and it was not something unique to my rebirther. I was beginning to see that the Babaji community was sizeable, and I learned more about an ashram in Colorado that was dedicated to the Divine Mother and Babaji's teachings. I knew instantly that I wanted to visit this special place.

The ashram was founded and is run based on the teachings of Babaji. The daily practice really spoke to me, and to this day I attempt to live my own life based on these principles. Life at the ashram begins early in the morning with a morning service called arati. This is a worship service welcoming the presence of the Divine; in it, light and incense are waved to Babaji and the Divine Mother. The flame symbolizes the removal of ignorance that exists between God and man.

The day comes to a close with bathing, followed by an evening arati service. The concept is that we give our days to God, start the day by inviting God's presence and end the day by giving thanks. They are bookends on the daily shelf of life, and everything is contained within those bookends. If we offer our daily work to God, there is nothing to carry over to the next day. This idea helps mediate modern anxieties and stress over work and societal challenges.

I loved the idea of a female representation of God in the form of the Divine Mother. It was an alien belief to me, but one that intrigued me. Even today, there are few feminine deities in the Western world. It is understandable, since our culture has traditionally been a patriarchal culture. The Divine Mother is the feminine presence of God that pervades the Universe. She is the energy that birthed us and continues to support us. She is the creator and the nurturer. She is the warrior and the destroyer. She is indescribable and called by many names. She is the transcendence of opposites. She has no beginning and no end. It is incomprehensible to attempt to imagine Her. She is associated with birth and death and transformation. She is the Earth Herself.

It has been said that the entire universe is reflected in one toenail on Her foot. How can we begin to grasp that? I have only been able to get a better understanding of Her by reading about the various Hindu goddesses, because each one represents a quality of the Divine Mother. Lakshmi is the goddess of abundance and good fortune, Saraswati is the goddess of language and expression and Kali is the goddess of death and rebirth. There are many other goddesses, but these may be the most well-known. All these qualities are aspects of the Divine Mother.

I can see now why I was drawn to Her. I had been looking for a mother figure for my entire life, and here was one in a form I might be able to relate to. She was the one to whom I could carry my burdens to lay at Her feet. She represented the love and compassion I had never known. At some level, maybe I also understood that the old patriarchal value of power and control needed to fall away and be replaced by a kinder, more feminine and compassionate way of living and relating. I know that for me personally, it was true. She gave me hope that we can enter a time of healing, love and respect for ourselves, each other and our Mother, the Earth. None of this was conscious for me at the time, but I was definitely being pulled toward a new feminine that would fill a void in my heart.

My first visit to the Haidakhandi Universal Ashram was certainly an adventure. I flew into Denver and then rented a car to drive the four hours to Crestone. At that time in the early 90s, the ashram was a small adobe-style temple located at the foot of the Sangre de Cristo mountain range. To get there required driving off the main road for 2 or 3 miles and then on an unfinished rutted road for another couple miles. It would have been difficult to find during daylight hours, but it was dark by the time I arrived in the village and there were no streetlights anywhere. At one point, I felt quite panicky, wondering whether I would be driving around these isolated roads indefinitely. I felt completely lost. It then occurred to me that I was making a pilgrimage of sorts, and it was very fitting for me. At that time, I felt lost in my life, and I had read enough about the spiritual path to understand that it is a road that is often treacherous or difficult and usually taken alone. My first drive to the ashram was a reminder of this, and I recognized I had to trust the journey and not panic or turn back.

I finally arrived at my destination and the evening devotional service of arati was just ending. I walked into the temple and was greeted by a large picture of Babaji, a 4-foot murti (statue) of the Divine Mother in all her resplendence as well as friendly, smiling faces. I immediately felt at home and wanted to cry.

The tears surprised me. What was I feeling? It was a sense of coming home, arriving at a place where I belonged and the recognition of that. It was connecting with a very ancient and powerful lineage that my soul knew well. It felt like I was being seen for who I was and loved and accepted for that reason alone. It was exactly how I had imagined it to be during my long search after leaving my childhood home.

It was an emotional arrival, and I was overcome with a profound sense of peace. I have arrived there so many times over the years, and my response is always the same. It is a respite from the chaos and stress of the outside world. It is a knowing that I am enveloped in the arms of Babaji and the Divine Mother, and I can finally collapse in this knowledge. It is simple and natural, and Babaji's presence there is palpable and enduring .

I recognized immediately that I had finally found my family of swans. I knew I belonged with Babaji and the Divine Mother at their home in the Colorado mountains.

The year of 2019 was the 30th anniversary of the installation of the Divine Mother statue that was enlivened at the ashram in 1989. This is a ceremony whereby the murti is pronounced "alive" and is treated as an embodied goddess. There is an early picture of Her on the temple wall, and I am always struck by how Her face has matured over the years—She has grown, as we have all grown.

For 32 years, She has been tenderly bathed and dressed in the early mornings and put to bed at night. She is also fed three organic, healthy meals every day. This is one of the main focuses of the ashram that captivated me. I was transfixed by the degree of love and attention that was given to Her. I remember thinking that if we could see our own inner goddess and treat Her with such love and respect, how much our lives would change. If we could do the same with other people, the world would also change.

Babaji referred to ashrams as islands in the sea of materialism. During the time He was in His body, He encouraged people to return home and create ashrams and centers throughout the world. According to the book *I Am Harmony*, Babaji told the author Radhe Shyam, "As there are islands in the sea, you should make ashrams in the ocean of the material world."[5] He went on to say that discipline is the most important aspect of ashram life. I imagine these "islands" to be islands of light shining in the darkness and beckoning those who have lost their way. My frequent visits to the Crestone ashram over the years have created in me a deeper understanding of a God-filled community where everyone works and prays together. It has become a solace for me where

I can escape periodically and recharge my depleted batteries after trying to cope with living in the material world.

Days at the ashram are spent practicing karma yoga. Babaji taught about the importance of this particular form of yoga. Karma yoga is the path of action and performing selfless service to the Divine. Babaji warned His followers frequently about the dangers of laziness and inaction. He taught that we should work hard every day, offer the fruits of our labor to God, and expect no outcome for ourselves. We are to work in love and harmony with each other. These are the fundamental living conditions at the ashram, where all visitors are expected to contribute daily by doing karma yoga and working side by side with other visitors. Babaji's words on karma yoga are: "Learn to talk less and work more. This is the field of spiritual practice. Karma is the highest way of perfection. . . . In the Gita (Bhagavad Gita), work is said to be the highest form of sadhana (daily spiritual practice)."[6]

I have visited my spiritual home most years since this initiation. During this time, I have watched the ashram grow in so many ways. As I said, my first trip revealed a small temple that could sit maybe 20 people. Since that time, many more buildings have been added and the temple has been made larger. There is now a dormitory, large kitchen, gift shop and residential living spaces. Many more people are being attracted to the ashram, and now hundreds may arrive for services and ceremonies. My spiritual family increases, and I'm enriched more and more as the years roll by.

A visit to the Divine Mother's ashram does not come without important lessons. In the beginning, there were multiple opportunities to learn more about myself and become more conscious. I remember having a dream one night that I had been asked to cut and sew a new gown for the Divine Mother. This was such an honor for me, and I wanted to make sure I did a first-class job. I was mortified in the dream when in error, I cut into the material in a way that made it unusable. I remember the feelings of shame and wanting to disappear before I had to own up to what felt like a mortal sin.

The next day, we were preparing for Navratri, which is a nine-day festival honoring the Divine Feminine. During this festival, the Divine Mother wears a new gown every day. I was horrified when Ramloti, the ashram director, placed sewing machines on the table and asked me to make one of the dresses. My worst fear came true as I reproduced the dream from the night before and cut into the material, rendering it useless. I learned two important lessons from this. Firstly, not everybody responds to mistakes the way my mother did, and secondly, my desire to do well and to be perfect was so strong that it caused me to make more mistakes.

There was another incident with Ramloti. I had made an appointment to have a massage in the village, and I believed I was breaking an unspoken rule by going for this massage. I thought that while I was on ashram property, I was to stay there and do my karma yoga and I was not allowed to leave the property. Like an errant child, I decided to keep my massage appointment secret so that I would not get into trouble. I left during personal time in the afternoon and had a wonderful massage. On the way back to the ashram, I came up with a plan to sneak into the dormitory and have a shower so I would be ready for the evening arati. Feeling immensely proud of myself for accomplishing this secret trip, I ran into the dormitory and straight into Ramloti, who was standing just inside the door. I was shocked and overcome with feelings of guilt as she asked me where I had been. I owned up to my actions and she said nothing. I was left with confusion around what had happened. I learned that I did not have to sneak around to do what I wanted to do, and after that, I always shared my plans with her and compromised if it was not a good time to be gone.

Another important lesson came from the flowers that were grown in the greenhouse. One of my favorite tasks was to pick flowers that would be offered to Babaji and the Divine Mother in the ceremonies. I found myself being very selective about the flowers I was choosing, and I was acutely aware of making sure I saved enough for the following day. When asked one time whether there were more flowers that could be used, I responded, "Yes, but then there would be none for tomorrow." It was a teachable moment when I was told, "There are always plenty of flowers for us. Mother is about abundance and always provides more than enough for our needs."

I went back and collected all the flowers that were blooming, and sure enough, there were just as many the next day. I realized that I had been living with an attitude of scarcity. I always saved good clothes for special occasions, used a fraction of whatever was available to me, had a fear of spending money and running out, and always thought there was never enough. This experience helped me realize that if we trust, we always have what we need. The Divine Mother is always taking care of us.

Early visits to the ashram also involved being told what to do by a myriad of people. Every time I was given work to do, I was rarely left alone, and people took it upon themselves to tell me how to do it and what I was doing wrong. I would follow one person's advice, and someone else would come along and tell me something completely different. I was reeling in confusion as I attempted to please everyone who came my way. I learned over time to listen to them but follow my own way or clarify with Ramloti about the best way to do it. This was a huge lesson in trusting my own ability and not blindly following instructions or trying to please other people.

The above examples are known as lilas, which are God's actions in human form. We can also see them in everyday life when we find ourselves in challenging relationships with others. They are like spiritual games played out between people and in certain situations so that we may learn life lessons and receive knowledge about ourselves. Because there are so many distractions in the everyday external world, we are not usually aware of them, but at the ashram and in silence, these games become obvious, creating a great opportunity to become clearer about the illusions we carry.

I have read many books about Babaji, written by people who were with him when He was in His body. I have also been fortunate to sit in a group and listen to others talk about their adventures in Haidakhan while they were with Him. They all recount how they learned their lessons from this great soul by the lilas He set up so they could clearly see themselves and their distorted thoughts. I know that the sneaking-around incident I related above helped me see immediately that I was carrying the belief that I had to hide things I wanted to do—and this thinking no longer served me.

I used to feel sad and sometimes jealous that I had never been with Babaji when He was in human form. I was 24 years old when He suddenly materialized, so He was alive during my lifetime. I used to ask myself how my life might have been different if I had been with Him while he was in His body. I then realized that Babaji's teachings and His energy have been handed down by the people who spent time with Him in India. I count my blessings that many of these people are still living and I can hear their stories firsthand. Even though I was never with Him, I acutely feel Babaji's presence—and He is a very real human form to me. His presence is even more powerful when a group of these older devotees get together and talk about Him.

It has now been almost 30 years since I first walked into the Crestone ashram and took my place at the table of the Babaji family. Throughout that time, He has woven His way through my life like the slender threads that Robert Johnson talks about in his memoir 'Balancing Heaven and Earth' which I mentioned in the introduction. He has been an eternal presence in the tapestry of my life. He has revealed Himself through occasional dreams when I am confused or grieving, but mostly He is a pervasive and trusted presence in my heart. I talk to Him daily and offer Him gifts of water, flowers, incense and fire.

One of the most beautiful and sustaining celebrations of ashram life is offering gifts to the Divine through the sacred fire, or yagna. When Babaji was in His body, He performed a small fire ceremony every morning outside His room. This practice was also followed by His close devotee and assistant, Muniraji, as he performed a small fire ceremony at his home every day. The fire ceremony is one of the main ceremonies at the Crestone ashram, where they make offerings to a small fire every morning and then a much larger fire on the days of the Full Moon and the New Moon.

It is a very ancient Vedic ritual in which the fire pit represents the mouth of the Divine. Offerings of milk, fruit, ghee (clarified butter), flowers, grains and incense are gently tossed into the fire as if we were feeding the Divine Mother Herself. This is done accompanied by spoken mantras in Hindi and Sanskrit. The symbolism connected to this is that we give back to the Divine Mother those things She has provided for us. In doing this, the fire creates smoke that rises to the heavens, then produces rains that fall upon the Earth and cause more fruit and grain to grow. It represents the sacred circle of life. The process of this raises the energetic vibration of the individuals who are offering, as well as the environment. It is therefore cleansing and healing to everyone who attends, as well as the physical surroundings.

I am not sure what draws me to the fire, except that it is like a magnet; that is, I feel mesmerized and awed by the power it represents. It speaks to me of the inner fire of passion and Divine Love. I understand through teachings and my own life experience that it demands the dross and ignorant aspects of ourselves be burned away until only Divine Love exists. That is the goal of the spiritual path: to realize the welding of Human and Divine Love, and to be one with God.

Dreams of the sacred fire and my relationship to it are dotted along my path like beacons of light on the darkest road. It has been a recurring theme for me in many of my dreams, and I have personally conducted small, personal fire ceremonies for myself and for other people over the last 25 years. The entire practice touches my heart, and when I offer the grains and flowers to the fire, I am connected to the sense of having done this for many years and many lifetimes. It provides me with continuity and a connection to another time and another realm. I am always astounded by the beauty of it.

This celebration also deepens my connection to God and Babaji. For many years, Ramloti has taken an annual trip to Florida. During this trip, she takes Babaji's padukas (sacred sandals) to each home as part of the festivities. These sandals are symbolic of Babaji's actual presence since He wore them when He was in his body. They hold His energy and are an important contribution to the worship services where they are adorned with perfume, flowers and a mala. Ramloti usually visits two or three devotees' homes and conducts a fire ceremony followed by kirtan (singing of special bhajans, or songs) and a potluck brunch. Friends and neighbors are invited to this gathering, as well as people we have never even met. It is always a high-energy occasion with special time spent with each other and with Baba. I have been fortunate enough to host one of these sacred fire ceremonies on these yearly visits. This is what I wrote as I prepared for this special visit one year:

Preparing to host the Sacred Fire for the first time in Jupiter, Florida, was like getting ready for a visit from Shri Babaji Himself. I spent weeks in a state of anxiety and excitement. I wanted everything to be perfect—the house had to be cleaned. A new havenkund (fire pit) was bought in His honor—the food had to be right and even a new patio was poured. The excitement seemed to be building every day.

Saturday came, and it seemed like a dream. I felt Baba's presence intensely, and it was a time of great joy and high energy. Every year is like this, but this year it felt so much more real—it was a preparation for His visit. Not only did I feel His presence personally, but it was a blessing to our new home and the community in which we live.'

I was reminded of the stories I had read about Babaji's travels in India. He frequently visited local towns and villages, and was followed by an entourage of people who wanted to travel with Him. The energy in Florida was like that, as many of us went on a tour of the homes where Ramloti was visiting and drove from different parts of Florida to celebrate and receive His blessings.

He did not have many general teachings but usually worked with everyone individually. However, the sacred fire was an integral part of His daily worship, and this has been handed down to His ashrams.

In addition to His encouragement to make karma yoga and the yagna part of our regular practice ,there were some major lessons He talked about often. They involved practical suggestions of how to live in a human world.

Truth, Simplicity and Love

These teachings are quite simple. Truth is to be honest and in a place of alignment with our words and our actions. It requires connecting with our deepest and most authentic Selves and speaking and acting from a place that is calm and peaceful.

Simplicity is living a simple life in harmony with Mother Earth and leaving a small carbon footprint. It requires detachment from the material world and a refusal to get overly involved with chaotic collective demands.

Love is the basis of all religions and the essence of everything. It is the ability to unconditionally love ourselves and all other sentient beings. It is being able to honor and respect all people and all of Mother Nature.

Follow the Religion That Is in Your Heart

Babaji did not support any one religion and said "There are many paths up the mountain," meaning all religions follow the same God and can be vehicles for God realization. He said His teachings were based on sharing a way of life based on the Sanatan Dharma, which was known as the Eternal Way. He advised that we follow the religion that is in our hearts and not shop religions. He stressed the importance of focusing on the one religious path we choose to follow.

One of my favorite stories about this is when He was visited at Haidakhan by men from the Sikh religion. They appeared before Him without their turbans, and Babaji asked them why they were not wearing them. They told him it was out of respect for Him. Babaji advised them to wear their turbans, and as support, He showed up the next day wearing a turban Himself. Babaji was more concerned that people live in harmony with each other than becoming divided by religion.

Religion and Spirituality

If you were planning to drive from New York to Los Angeles, there are many different routes you could take. You could do it in the shortest possible time and be delayed by heavy traffic or car problems, or you could meander and take several interesting detours along the way. If you keep your eye on the goal (getting to California), you will eventually arrive. In the same way, if you are focused on knowing God, there are many different avenues to get you there. Each path represents a different religion that will lead you to God. Babaji's teachings to follow the religion that is in your heart signify that we should align ourselves to a religion that connects us to God in a heart-felt way.

I was raised in the Episcopalian or Anglican faith and was baptized in the church and confirmed when I was 13 years old. My parents never encouraged me to go to church, and neither did they discourage me. The only time I ever saw them attend was for weddings and funerals. The school I attended taught the Bible and had a daily worship service with hymns and readings from the Old and New Testaments. For some of my early teenage years, I attended church and then confirmation classes with my friends. It was my decision to do both, and my parents seemed not to care about my choices.

While my friends and I became well versed in the Bible and enjoyed raucously singing various hymns, I never found God in the church. Our church dated back to medieval times, and while it was a beautiful and picturesque building, it was cold and damp inside and left me feeling disconnected and alienated from my picture of the jolly old Santa Claus–like man I imagined God to be. It was not long before I decided I would not go to church on a regular basis.

I am still drawn to the mystery of the Eucharist, however, and to the rituals practiced by the church. There is something about these practices that is poignant and reminds me of my childhood, humility and Divine connection. This is especially true during Easter and Christmas, when I still occasionally enjoy attending a Christian service.

It is important to realize that any religious doctrine involves God. I believe we should strive to form a personal relationship with God, so it only makes sense that if we follow a religion, it should be one that draws us into His loving arms. If the doctrine does not feel nurturing and loving, then maybe you are in the wrong place.

If you choose to follow a religion, then the religion becomes your guru in a sense, since you accept and follow all the dogma that is attached to it. Spirituality provides us more freedom to find our own way. It is like having access to many different buffet tables from which we can select food, while religion offers us only one table. There may be a temptation to hop from one table to another without really developing our personal relationship. I think that's what Babaji was addressing when He said to stay with one guru.

My own history has been built on my Episcopalian roots, so that has been a strong foundation to my belief in God and Christ. Many find it difficult to believe that I have a guru and yet I believe in Christ, but how could I not? The more we open ourselves to understanding, the greater our vision can be.

Babaji often spoke symbolically through His actions and said very little in words. He left it to each individual to learn the lessons He was showing them. One way He illustrated that we should live in harmony was via the following story: Two women were sitting next to each other; one had blonde hair and the other had dark hair. Babaji began to silently plait strands of the dark hair and light hair together so they were joined inextricably.

Mahakranti

Babaji frequently predicted the coming of a spiritual revolution, which He referred to as Mahakranti. In July 1979, He said, "In the aftermath of the revolution—which will be total; no country big or small, will be spared—some countries will be totally erased, leaving no sign of their existence. In some, three to five percent of the population will be spared and will survive," and, "The destruction will be brought about by earthquakes, floods, accidents, collisions and wars..." He later talked about the necessity to wipe out corruption: "The leaders of all countries are busy safeguarding their positions and have totally ignored their people's needs and interests. These leaders are misguiding the public...New leaders are being trained and prepared to take over from the corrupt leaders. The new leaders will restore justice and proper order and bring peace."[7]

He saw this as a necessary spiritual revolution because people have lost their way. He predicted that it would take ten years for this revolution to be complete, and it would result in peace. He foresaw this happening in the 1980s, but many say that 2020 and all the chaos that has surrounded us is the beginning of the Mahakranti.

He told the people in Haidakhan that, as his devotees, we should be prepared for this revolution, which will affect the entire world. He said we must bring alertness into our lives, so we are ready to face it with courage and with a willingness to give up our lives. He said, "When unrighteousness prevails in the world, this is the only path possible."[8]

On Nonviolence

Babaji's teachings on nonviolence are interesting because He constantly said He had no time for nonviolence. He urged people to be brave and alert and have courage to do the right thing. He said, "I want to make everybody brave. Man's blood has become like water. So many atrocities are done, and people let them happen in the name of nonviolence. Nonviolence is not for this."[9]

Later, He said "Nonviolence itself is now contaminating the world. . . . Babaji wants some violent people so that others may grow in wisdom and discrimination and learn to make decisions."[10] It sounds contradictory for Him to teach on the one hand peace and harmony and then on the other to condemn nonviolence. I think He is saying that we must be alert and prepared to fight for the truth and for goodness. It is only when we have wiped out evil that we can achieve peace and harmony.

I am a mirror

Listening to a group of older devotees who were with Babaji when He was in His body, I was reminded about how Babaji appeared differently to different people at the same time. At any given moment, one person may have seen Him as stern while another saw Him as loving or playful. I heard that in a glance, a devotee might see Him morph into many different forms of the Divine, changing in seconds. It was like a slide show of images through Babaji's body of Gods and Goddesses. Visitors to His ashram saw themselves reflected back by Him and in that way they were able to understand how they might change their thoughts or perception of themselves and the people around them. Babaji himself said *'I am the mirror, in which you can see yourself. I am like fire; don't stay too far away or you won't get the warmth: but don't come too close least you get burnt.'*[11] This parallels Jung's concept of projection where we see the unwanted parts of ourselves in others.

I can see how Jung's beliefs and this ancient Indian faith are woven together with a shared understanding. Jung had introduced the idea of symbolism to me and set me on a path of symbolic thinking. I was then led to this rich spiritual tradition, which was steeped in symbolism. As I learned more about the gods and goddesses of India, I learned more about God and also more about myself. I saw parts of myself reflected in them. My fire and passion were reflected by Kali, while I also noted the strength of Durga and the wisdom of Saraswati in myself. Ganesh became my constant guide as I prayed to Him to remove the obstacles in my life.

My concept of God changed as I realized that God was both male and female and contained all the qualities of all the gods and goddesses that I was learning about. God cannot be imagined, because S(He) is beyond the imagination. It was the feminine side of God that captured me the most. I had grown up with the idea of a masculine God, which aligned with a patriarchy that has been running the Western world for all time. At the same time I was learning about accepting and valuing my feminine side as a woman through Marion Woodman's books, I was learning about the Divine Mother through the ashram and the Hindu scriptures.

We need the presence of the Divine Mother in our world today, and my growing love for Her made me more aware of our environment and how She is being polluted by our thoughtlessness. I needed Her compassion and love in my life and realized just how much the world needs it, too. She became a model to me and the mother I never had. It was no accident that She arrived on the scene to help me understand Her contribution and to help heal my early wounds.

Notes

[1] *Shastriji, Haidakhandi Sapta Sati*, pp. 182.

[2] Ibid., p. 228

[3] Clarissa Pinkola Estes, *Women who run with the Wolves*, p. 172.

[4] Shdema Goodman, *Babaji—Meeting with Truth*, pp. 36-37.

[5] Radye Shyam, *I am Harmony*, p. 294.

[6] Haidakhandi Samaj, *The Teachings of Babaji*. p. 25.

[7] Radye Shyam, *I am Harmony*. p. 264.

[8] Haidakhandi Samaj, *Teachings of Babaji*. p. 61.

[9] Ibid., p. 25.

[10] Ibid., p. 29.

[11] G.Reichel Verlag, *Babaji—Message from the Himalayas*, p. 102.

Personal Thoughts

PART 4
BODY AS HOME

Without the metaphor, the mind may be fed, but the imagination and the heart go hungry. Without the pondering in the soul, the banquet table in dreams may be laden, but the food cannot be assimilated and so the soul starves.[1]

—*The Ravaged Bridegroom—Masculinity in Women,*
by Marion Woodman: Inner City Books

14.
BODYSOUL RHYTHMS®

While my inner structure was being rebuilt and I was feeling deeply supported on my spiritual path, I still felt there was something missing. I was now working as a Licensed Clinical Social Worker and traveling to be with my Babaji family in Colorado at least once a year. I had settled into a new normal. Tom and I were now grandparents, and we were spending many happy times with our granddaughter, Lexi, who was around five years old. She would come and spend Friday nights with us, and I have many great memories of taking her to the mall and the botanical gardens and eating Chinese food at our favorite restaurant.

My inner focus was still on Babaji and what I saw as my spiritual world. I was still trying to make sense of the incident that catapulted me into this period of psychological and spiritual upheaval. I desperately wanted to recreate the experience that took me to nirvana before smashing me onto the rocks below. Nirvana was now light years away and utterly elusive. I continued with my daily practice of meditation and puja and would occasionally hold a small sacred fire at my home, but I still wanted the high that was created at that special time.

Sometimes it is the mundane and ordinary that speaks to us the loudest. We can live with it for years, and then suddenly we really notice that which we had taken for granted. It shoots into our awareness like a meteor. It was that way for me.

For these eight years following my glimpse of heaven, I was still reading Marion's books and reading Jungian psychology. The year 1999 quickly arrived and changed my life yet again. It was an introduction to my body and my relationship to it. I was to meet it head on.

The body is a receptacle for all the parts of ourselves we deem unacceptable. It is therefore the storehouse of pain and trauma. It is a physical living proof of the existence of our shadow. The last decade or so has revealed a growing collection of literature about the connection between our body and our emotions. Candace Pert was a pioneer when she wrote *Molecules of Emotion in 1997* and revealed that every cell of the body has its own consciousness or mind. As a neuroscientist, she introduced the concept of a body mind that connects the body and emotions.[2]

Marion Woodman was also on the frontier of these beliefs and went on to teach about the use of dream symbols in the body to promote energetic and physical healing. Marion had become a Jungian analyst in the second half of her life after teaching high-school English. I knew nothing about her until I read and re-read *The Pregnant Virgin*. I then read every book she ever wrote at that time.

In her books, she talks about how the patriarchy has dominated our nation and our lives for generations, and how, as women, our upbringing has cut us off from ourselves and our feminine principles. She suggests there is a male and female component within every person, and their ultimate desire is to come together. She describes how we can utilize our dreams in order to understand our psyches and receive guidance from our souls.

I was mesmerized by her words, and her ideas resonated deeply with me. The effect of her writing was that I was sitting down to listen to an intimate friend and mentor. She was a pioneer as a teacher of the feminine principle and the concept of discovering our own authenticity as women.

The idea of healing our wounded inner feminine and creating a new inner masculine who will cherish and support these feminine principles speaks to me even more these days. I am beginning to see this occur on a collective level as the old patriarchy is threatened. I believe that the old masculine principles of power and corruption are falling away and will be replaced by a kinder, more feminine and compassionate way of living and relating. As Babaji predicted when he talked about the Revolution, this will ultimately be a time of healing, leading to greater peace and harmony and more love and respect for the feminine within ourselves, each other and the world. There will also be a deeper respect for Mother Earth and more courage to go out into the world to share our gifts in the larger community.

Being drawn to Marion through her books caused me to investigate whether she was conducting any workshops, and I was excited to learn that she was offering week-long intensives with two other women, Mary Hamilton and Anne Skinner. The first workshop I attended was on Gabriola Island in British Columbia, Canada. It was a beautiful island, accessible only by ferry or seaplane, and the perfect setting for exploring nature and our own BodySoul connection, both internally and externally.

Marion, Mary and Anne had developed a body of work called BodySoul Rhythms®, which involved exploring dreams in the mornings and followed by body work, mask-making and voice work in the afternoons and evenings. It was based on the premise that Body and Soul are one and the same, and unresolved trauma is stored in the cells of the body. Using images from our dreams, we are able to access these areas of trauma and release the energy that is stored there. By doing this, we also release, emotionally and spiritually.

We created masks that represented the energy that lay dormant within us and wanting to be lived. There was a way that the masks created themselves from the dream images. It was liberating and frightening to wear these masks and utilize their energies, which became the impetus for new life. It took us most of the week to create the masks, and we would gather in the evenings to paint and decorate them according to our inner promptings, which came from our dreams and our movements. We often had no idea what would emerge at the end of the week, which culminated in a gathering for the entire group where we wore our masks and interacted with each other. It was quite astonishing to recognize how much our movement and behavior changed as we actively lived out the energies behind our masks.

Over the course of my work with Marion, I made three masks. The first was a firebird with brilliant red feathers and a long beak. The firebird is a beautiful magical bird with red, orange and yellow feathers that glow like fire. He is found in many Russian fairy tales and is usually involved in a mythical quest in which part of his plumage is found by someone who sets off on a journey to find the owner of this magnificent feather. Somehow, this captivating bird spoke to me and found his way into one of my masks. I am just now realizing how appropriate this was, as I had spent so many years searching for a repetition of being rocketed to the heavens during that rebirthing experience in 1991.

I can remember at the mask party desperately trying to soar up into the heights where this bird wanted to fly and where he really belonged. I recognized that my human body could barely get off the ground. I found myself flapping from one corner of the room to another, like a terrified chicken, and never approaching the image that was in my imagination. It was a moment of truth that I am only now fully realizing. We are constrained by our human body in ways we may never know. Artists and writers and athletes come close to this awareness when they are unable to find the right words or actions for their images or when the reality of their art falls short of their inner visions.

After my experience with this mask, I went on to create a mask of the Green Man and a young seven-year-old red-headed boy who just wanted to go fishing. The Green Man is another archetypal figure who has been around for centuries, especially in Europe. He represents oneness with the earth and is portrayed on many old buildings in the United Kingdom as a huge face covered in leaves and foliage. He, together with my red-headed fisherman, illustrate my psyche attempting to reconcile the spiritual aspect of me represented in the firebird with the grounding of the mortal body in the Earth. Again, none of this was conscious at the time, but now I see that my soul needed to make this reconciliation.

It is impossible to describe exactly what happened during these retreats, and I can only liken it to what it may have been like to participate in the Eleusinian mysteries or go to the temple of Asklepios, the Greek god of healing. In those ancient times, people would travel from all over for healing of physical, emotional and psychological disorders. They would be required to sleep overnight in the temple and undergo a procedure where the gods were invoked to appear with healing messages in their dreams. In the same way, BodySoul Rhythms® teaches us how to use our dream images as healing poultices for our bodies and souls.

After this initial workshop, I completed more and then applied for Marion's leadership training program. This was a three-year program in which approximately 40 women from around the globe participated. We were required to attend regular workshops in Canada and assist staff in at least one of them. To say that these retreats were easy and looked forward to with great anticipation would not be true. I always went with great inner resistance and a high level of anxiety, but once there, the cells of my body absorbed Marion's words as quickly and greedily as parched seedlings would respond to water. They were rich nourishment physically, emotionally and spiritually. I am sure that the resistance was fear of the unknown. Sinking deep into my body during the middle of each week was like falling through cobwebs to every cell within me, and wondering whether I would ever find my way back from a place that was unfamiliar and sometimes chaotic. I always emerged, every time with a treasure or gift that I had discovered about myself during the process. I often felt as if I had shed many layers of skin during the week and returned home feeling lighter in every way.

Although I was not always consciously aware of the changes within, I knew that some inner movement was taking place, and today, seeing the evolution of my masks validates that. Even now, I cannot comprehend or verbalize exactly what happened and the results of the body work that took place then are still seeping into my conscious mind. The changes were subtle and continue to this day.

While I never had a personal relationship with Marion, she was very generous with her time and would sometimes invite us to her home for a lecture or discussion. We grew to know her quite well, which was a blessing. She was a real character with a wicked sense of humor. She loved poetry and the classics and would quote from Shakespeare and all the great poets, one of her favorites being Emily Dickinson. She had a gaze like my grandmother's. It was as if she could see through the veils and also into the depths of who we were. She was honest and authentic and had no time for sentimentality. In her book, *The Ravaged Bridegroom*, she writes, "Sentimentality not only keeps the anger at a distance, it also betrays genuine feeling."[3]

She also had a gift for working with women in a group, keeping us on task with our personal work while helping us build a strong, supportive container. I often think that, for many of us, she was the mother we never had. She was, however, a transitional mother, because from her, I learned that I had spent most of my life looking for this mother in numerous other women, and now I was faced with the knowledge that I had to ultimately learn to mother myself.

Great teachers have the ability to transmit knowledge and wisdom to their students energetically, either through personal relationship or from a distance. Sometimes, as I sat in front of her on the floor while she was talking, I would feel disoriented and a little faint. I would then realize it was due to the intense vibration that was rolling off her as she talked. Like a magnet picking up metal filings, she was able to radiate healing energy that transformed all who entered her field. Maybe she was able to tap into a higher vibrational frequency as she recited verses of poetry, shared wisdom from famous literature and spoke truths with which we all resonated.

Arnold Mindell, in his book *Dreambody*, may have a scientific reason for this phenomenon when he describes the dreambody (which is also known as the subtle body), as an energetic field or vibration. He states "the flow and rhythm of the dreambody constitute a 'field' experience. . . . The field is a definite sensation of one's self as a process with only vague extremities in time and space."[4]

Maybe this is what we call "being in the zone" when we refer to athletes who align their psyches with their bodies so perfectly that they have instances of achieving great heights in their chosen sport.

Whatever it was, Marion was illustrating the power that can be generated when we speak from the depths of our soul.

Notes

[1] Marion Woodman. *The Ravaged Bridegroom—Masculinity in Women*, p. 27.

[2] Candace Pert, Azquotes, last accessed February 13, 2021, azquotes.com/author/24367-Candace_Pert.

[3] Marion Woodman, *The Ravaged Bridegroom—Masculinity in Women*, p. 154.

[4] Arnold Mandell, *Dreambody—The Body's role in revealing the Self*, p. 14.

Personal Thoughts

Our soul requires dedication to doing what we love and loving what we do. Like a fine wine that improves with age, it will respond to this joyfully with wisdom and guidance. Care for your soul as you would care for the Divine Mother herself because you are eternally connected to Her.

—Elaine Heroux

15.
SOUL SEASONING

This was a time of deep inner healing, soul awakening and soul seasoning. Through the body work, I was able to connect to the deep rage and grief I had been carrying toward my mother. With encouragement, I was able to express these emotions, and that was the beginning of healing the gulf between my mother and myself that I had felt since my early adulthood.

Working with our bodies on the floor and uncovering our emotional and energetic blocks, allowed us to discover more of who we were. We learned that the body is a mediator between spirit and matter. Spirit is outside the body and has a masculine element in that it can strike us suddenly and memorably. My rebirthing experience came from the world of spirit and had the result of ravishing me, much in the way we can be ravished in a romantic situation. The results are similar and include instantly feeling in love and enveloped in something we have no power over.

It is not surprising that the great mystics wrote about their connection with the Divine in the same way they would write about a passionate love experience. Soul, on the other hand, is within the body. For me, my soul was reignited by the union of spirit and matter during my rebirthing experience. I believe that the soul can go into hiding as a way to deal with traumatic experiences. I never became aware of my own soul until I started working with Marion. She helped me understand that soul is our own personal aspect of spirit. It is embodied spirit. I can see now that I became intrigued by the allure of spirit from an early age, but it was only when I found Marion that I discovered my body and soul.

The body houses the soul. Marion describes it this way:

Spirit yearns with limitless aspirations; matter imposes limitations on spirit. Soul mediates between them. When spirit is brought down by nature, soul suffers. When opaque matter is brought into consciousness, soul suffers. The function of soul growth is suffering and sacrifice. In confronting the disasters of spirit, we come to terms with limitations. That is the intermediate world. . . . Journeying between earth and heaven, joining one to the other, the soul understands the language of poetry, the language of metaphor, which integrates the image with feeling, mind and imagination. The metaphor, or the symbol, heals because it speaks to the TOTAL person. For this reason, Jung believed that the contemplation of dream images was the pathway to wholeness.[1]

Do you remember the poor boy who shattered his gift for his mother before he could get it home, and his mother's reaction of laughing about it? I received a clear understanding of why this bothered me so much from one of Marion's stories. She told about a young boy who came home late from school because he had stopped by the river and found some beautiful stones. Filling his pocket with them, he ran home excitedly to give them to his mother as a gift. The following was her reaction: "She was furious with him and turned him upside down and shook him, and the stones went all over. 'Now pick them up,' she told him, 'and throw them out in the lane where they belong.'" Marion went on to say it was traumatic for the boy because "he truly loved those stones. They had a numinosity for him, and his mother had no sense at all he was offering his soul to her."[2]

Obviously, from an early age, I had an unconscious understanding of soul and the ability to see the symbolic meaning of situations that others around me could not see. This innate sense became buried in me as I proceeded to focus on the world of spirit. Marion helped me to uncover this gift and recognize the qualities of soul. These workshops were a time of rich nourishment for this very personal inner spiritual home.

The years I spent with Marion, Anne and Mary and the other BodySoul participants was a special era in my life that yielded important major gifts. The first was that I learned to put my experiences of the spirit realm into better perspective. My encounters with spirit from years before were like glimpsing the light in the heavens above before they dropped to the mud at the bottom of the stream. It was a fall from ecstasy to depression, and there was no in between. BodySoul was an encounter with my own body, my Self, and the beginning of knowing who I was and developing my own soul, or the essence of me.

I began to feel more grounded than I had ever felt, and I learned tools that would balance the spiritual and the human, the body and the soul. For the three years I participated in this program, I began to heal my own body and emotions and learned to trust in my body home and the images and intuition that emanated from it. With that came the ability to be more spontaneous and accepting.

The space Marion, Anne and Mary created was sacred and solid. It was a huge gift to work with a group of 40 women over three years, and to know we all supported each other in this work. There was a deep trust and safety that we'd collectively created. I often thought it strange that I did not form many lasting intimate friendships with these women although we were coming together at a very deep level in community growth. I knew, however, that we would always be connected and supported due to the work we were doing and the strength of the container/safety net that was formed and held by the leaders and each other.

I cannot say enough about the importance of the container. It was an essential contributor to my new experience of feeling grounded. The grounding came not only from the safety of the workshops, but also from the theoretical underpinnings of Jung, which provided the psychological and spiritual framework. This was the outer container. Jungian psychology was large enough to hold the transpersonal as well as the personal, leading me to be able to integrate both of these aspects of myself.

There were two memorable instances I carry to this day, as they were moments that changed my life and the way I looked at things. Both involved my dreams. In the first, I dreamed I was at a BodySoul gathering and Marion was trying to decide whether she would go and work in Hawaii. The ending of the dream saw me leaving the gathering and noticing that Marion was playing a piano by the door when I was on my way out. I presented this dream to Marion the following day and she said, "Elaine, you are psychic!" It turns out she had been trying to make a decision about whether to go to Hawaii to offer a workshop. She also said that she did, in fact, play the piano. This was a huge validation for me that I did have psychic abilities. It also opened a discussion in the room when many women shared that they, too, have had psychic experiences. After that incident, I felt seen and heard and marginalized myself less because of my connections to the world of spirit.

The second dream was actually a nightmare. In the dream, I was standing in line with a group of people waiting to be decapitated. It was terrifying as the line slowly moved me forward and I knew that I would be beheaded on a copy machine. My anxiety was still high as I went into the community room that day. I was relieved when Marion asked me to share my dream. As I re-lived the horror of it, she looked at me with her penetrating eyes and said, "But Elaine, the head has to come off'."

She then went on to say that we must sacrifice our heads and intellects so we can be directed by our hearts. I instantly recognized the truth of this and saw the irony that the dream world would present an important piece of wisdom in such a shocking and scary form. I was learning never to take a dream literally, because often, a nightmare carries the greatest gifts and does it in a horrifying manner that will get our attention. Also, we will often find villains who are chasing us in our dreams, but upon further investigation, we may discover that these villains are allies trying to get our attention and tell us about something important.

This incident brought back memories of leaving the ARE group when I realized there was no heart connection for me. Babaji came into my life soon after that, tossing me onto a path of truth, simplicity and love. It was the beginning of a journey to learn to connect to my heart, and this dream was yet another reminder of that.

I learned that Marion also had an Indian connection and had traveled to India where she had a near-death experience. In *The Pregnant Virgin*, she wrote about traveling to India to find God in an ashram and how she'd ended up almost dying in a hotel room.³ India was the initiation into a new life for her in the same way that Babaji, my Indian guru, was an initiation for me. They were both periods of rebirth. I feel that Babaji was guiding me and leading me to deeper understanding through Marion's words.

Babaji and the Divine Mother were always present at these workshops, in which Marion would set up an altar at the beginning of the week to acknowledge the feminine presence of God in the form of Sophia. The altar would be opened with a prayer each morning and was a constant reminder of a power at work that was greater than ourselves. There were always beautiful flowers on the altar, as well as a collection of meaningful pictures and keepsakes that we brought with us. The invoked presence of Sophia each day, as well as Marion's teachings about feminine psychology, was totally aligned with my knowledge and experience of the Divine Mother and other Hindu goddesses. This was yet another level of containment. I was enveloped in an environment that was teaching about the love and value of the Divine Feminine, and this was accompanied by a trustworthy source of psychological theory. This was a world of love and compassion, trust and vulnerability, which also included developing authenticity, personal strength and power. There was a very organic and seamless combination of my spiritual life with Babaji, my understanding of Jungian psychology and my continued search for myself, as a woman, with Marion.

This became an ideal crucible in which I felt safe and free to explore my emotions, my body and my inner images.

During this time, I learned that our bodies are the vehicles that carry us through life. When I say "learned," I mean that I understood this to be true down to the very cells of my body. Learning through the body is different from the traditional form of learning that comes from the head. I can learn something academically, but I don't know it to be true for me until I feel it resonate in my body. Our bodies are our human homes, and as such, they require love, care and respect. They also hold immense wisdom and guidance. They are the containers for our own personal spirit or soul. This can be fed by dream images, painting, poetry, literature, music and other arts.

This dream world is in contact with both the spirit world and the physical world and is very fertile ground for healing, both physically and psychologically. We can see it as a membrane through which unconscious messages are sent from the body to the spirit and healing messages can be sent from the spirit to the body. Marion explains how she healed herself of cancer by focusing on these messages and doing exercises where, in her imagination, she placed healing images in the diseased area of her body and breathed into them on a daily basis. She describes the images as acting as transformers, accessing healing energy from the spirit and using it to heal blocked energy in the body.[4]

Our personal images add depth and meaning to our lives, and without them, life would be intolerable. We would solely live a concrete black-and-white existence. Can you imagine a life without the arts? Music, art, writing and creativity are all inhabitants of our dream world. They allow us to play with our images and find a medium of expression. They assist with our healing and frequently provide solace in a troubled family or troubled world.

Dreams can show us a picture of our perceptions. They reveal shadow aspects of ourselves that we are unaware of. In this way, they can help us correct any unconscious beliefs we may be acting from. They also remind us when it is time to refocus our attention. Soul is also nourished by our environment and doing what we love. As the soul is fed, it becomes mature and seasoned, like a fine wine, and begins to shine through the faces that we turn out to the world. It informs our entire life. It is wise to exercise discrimination and be mindful about the feeding of our souls, because the reverse can be true. If we feed it negativity and pain, our soul will fail to thrive.

During this time, I came to a recognition that I was psychic and had experienced communications from the world of spirit, but I was also a soul in a human body—and in order to have a happy life, I was being called to live fully in my body, with the pain and the joy that came with that. I was now more aware of the beauty and mystery of life and my own personal contribution to it. I was no longer looking outside myself for answers.

In Patricia Reis's book, *Daughters of Saturn*, she says that one of the steps toward autonomy in women is the necessity for them to go through what she calls the *Wildzone*. She describes this as a place "where we begin to move deeply into our bodies to discover and live our wildish nature." She says it is a place "where women find the ground they can stand upon," and "where we get our bodies back" and from where "we define ourselves." It is a space for women only. She concludes that, "For women today going into our 'wildness' means entering a new dimension of space and time, feeling our connection to all living things, and learning to live our lives from that place of knowing."[5]

In hindsight, I can say that participating in BodySoul workshops was entering the Wildzone, with many of the consequences Reis outlines above. Now, 20 years later, I am realizing that the work continues to work on me, as it weaves itself through the cells of my body. It was as if the mystery that is the psyche was ignited and continues to burn. More and more of my decisions are made from this place, and I am gaining greater trust in it. I am now able to put that period of my life into a broader perspective as I see that really living in my body on a daily basis was able to help me reconcile the enormous gulf within my psyche between the spirit world and the mortal world. I learned how to come home to my body.

Notes

[1] Marion Woodman, *The Ravaged Bridegroom—Masculinity in Women*, Inner City Books, p. 27.

[2] Ibid, *Conscious Femininity*, Inner City Books, p. 75.

[3] Ibid., *The Pregnant Virgin*, Inner City Books, pp. 175-183.

[4] Ibid., *Marion Woodman Foundation BodySoul Rhythms® Leadership Training Workshops*.

[5] Patricia Reis, *Daughters of Saturn*, pp. 188-189.

Personal Thoughts

PART 5
FOLLOW YOUR DESTINY

It is already becoming clear that a chapter which had a Western beginning will have to have an Indian ending if it is not to end in the self-destruction of the human race. At this supremely dangerous moment in history, the only way of salvation for mankind is the ancient Hindu way, there we have the attitude and spirit that can make it possible for the human race to grow together in to a single family.[1]

—Dr Arnold Toynbee

16.
INDIA CALLS

Many years ago, when I was in my 20s, I had a recurring dream. I was on an elevator and trying to find the 17th floor. It kept stopping on another floor, and the door would open. Outside was a world of bright color and noise, and women in beautiful saris walked by. In the dream, I made myself a mental note to come back to this floor, because the world outside was intriguing and vibrant. I would press the button for the 17th floor again, and once more it would start to move up but then return to the scene of India. My rational mind was looking for something I had lost at age 17, but my soul knew better what my destiny would be.

This dream was a premonition of sorts, because when Babaji came into my life, I was introduced to India and her culture. Little did I know when I had that dream that I would have an Indian guru and take a trip to India in 2009.

Going to India and the Babaji ashram in Haidakhan had been a fantasy of mine since my early visits to the Crestone ashram. It was a fantasy I never really expected to become reality. Maybe I didn't feel I deserved for my dreams to come true, so I sabotaged them with my negative thoughts. I realized later that I had a few of these desires locked away. They were like special gifts that were put on top shelves and saved for special occasions, or favorite clothes that were left hanging in the closet for a memorable event. Of course, they were never used, but as long as I knew they were there, they became a comfort in my inner life when I could take them out and look at them occasionally. I think this represents the depth of my poverty consciousness. I really believed that happiness and abundance were limited and so scarce that I had to store good things for a rainy day.

At that time, there was an important woman I used to speak with on the telephone about my dreams. She had been recommended to me by Marion, and I had never met her. Her name was Patricia Reis, and she is the author of the book *Daughters of Saturn*. I would share my dreams with her, and she would help me understand what they might be telling me. I trusted and valued this woman and could not believe how she seemed to get me without having met me or been around me in person.

One day in 2009 as I was recounting one of my sacred fire dreams to her, she asked, "What is this about India and the sacred fire?"

I then explained that this was an important aspect of my spiritual life and close to my heart. She responded, "Elaine, you have to go to India—it is your spiritual destiny." As she said these words, they resonated so deeply with me that, at that very moment, I made the decision to go. I knew without a shadow of a doubt that she was right. I began planning immediately and prepared to go for Spring Navratri.

Navratri is a special celebration in the Hindu calendar celebrating nine days of the Divine Feminine. At the ashram, the feminine is represented by the goddesses Durga, Lakshmi and Saraswati. Each goddess is celebrated for three days that are rich in symbolism. Durga represents the destruction of what no longer works, Lakshmi welcomes the new and fruitful into our lives and Saraswati represents the wisdom that is shared with the world. These nine days are always a special time of reading sacred texts, praying, singing and attending daily fire ceremonies.

I asked Tom if he would come with me, knowing that he would refuse. This was not his path or his dream, and I knew it. While it would have been great for us to go together, I also respected and understood his unwillingness to be involved. He was already stretching out of his comfort zone when he agreed to host the yearly sacred fire ceremony in our home. I knew his destiny was not my destiny.

He was obviously concerned about my taking a solitary trip to India and he expressed this, but it was ultimately my decision and he accepted it. Marion, in her writing about seeing her husband with no projections, touches me at a personal level when she says, "God knows I've made him suffer and he's made me suffer. But we're here."[2]

The same can be said of my relationship with Tom. We have both caused suffering to the other through decisions we have made, but we have also supported each other's unique destiny—and it is through that suffering that a tender, deeper love was born.

I have frequently been asked questions about Tom and my spiritual path. People have asked, "Is your husband on the same spiritual path as you?" When I tell them no, there is a silent judgment or question that hangs in the air, which I sometimes feel urged to defend. Sometimes, people will even tell me they could never be in a relationship with someone who does not share their spiritual beliefs. I believe there is a collective idea that intimate relationships will not work if you are not both following the same spiritual path. This is nonsense. Tom and I shared the same values, a few of which were kindness, acceptance, integrity, respect, honesty and a fierce desire to be our own person.

In addition to shared values, there are ways that each partner can complement the other, which happened in our marriage. I frequently saw Tom as an enormous rock in the middle of the ocean. I was a bird that would take off toward the horizon, and I always returned, bringing nourishment for both of us and knowing that he would remain steadfastly there. Tom was my anchor and my grounding, and I recognized and accepted this. I didn't always like it, because he could bring me down to Earth with one thoughtful sentence. I knew, however, that there was wisdom in his words I needed to listen to. We also had so many things in common and enjoyed sharing books, playing golf and watching basketball and golf on TV. I like to think we both contributed to each other and that he benefited from my contribution of an otherworldly view of life as much as I benefited from his realism.

There were some people I knew in the Babaji community who went to the Indian ashram every year, and I knew I could have chosen to go with them. Instead, I chose to go alone. I didn't want the comfort and safety of a group; I wanted this to be my own personal experience with Babaji. I spent a great deal of time preparing and talking to friends who had gone before me. They helped me decide on important items to take, how to pack lightly and how to get to the Haidakhan ashram. I am indebted to Ramloti at the Crestone ashram for helping me plan ahead, arranging a place to stay in Delhi, purchasing rail tickets in advance and so much more.

There was a funny learning experience that happened over clothes she had sent me to take to India. A package of beautiful Indian punjabi suits arrived for me to wear on my trip. A punjabi suit is a three-piece woman's outfit that consists of a tunic, balloon-type pants and a large shawl. They are usually made of brightly colored material, and the top is covered in glittering mirrors and sequins. I prefer to wear these over a sari ,which I find difficult to wrap and wear comfortably.

I was thrilled with these clothes and couldn't wait to try them on. As the time for my trip grew closer, I obsessively began asking myself such questions as: *Am I taking enough clothes? Do I have everything I need, or have I forgotten anything? And do I need a key for my suitcase?*

Losing all my beautiful new clothes through theft was my main concern. One day, I verbalized this worry to Ramloti and she responded, "Elaine, they all belonged to other people—you did not pay for them and they are of no monetary value. What does it matter if you lose them all?"

This suddenly shocked me into the realization that I was speaking from the place of scarcity I had become so accustomed to. I then saw the funny side of it—that I could put so much energy into worrying about something so unimportant. Sometimes, people can say something that appears to have great shock value which results in our being shaken loose of the delusion we are carrying. That was one of those moments for me.

Finally, the day arrived that I was to leave. It seemed as if I had awaited this moment for an eternity, and now it was really happening. I flew out of Miami with a layover in Amsterdam and arrived at Delhi Airport late at night. Arrangements had been made for me to take a cab to the home of some friends of Ramloti, where I was going to spend a night before leaving for Haidakhan.

By the time I had secured my cab and reached their home, it was about 1 or 2 a.m. My initiation to India came at this unearthly hour of the morning when, debilitated by jet lag and lack of sleep, I could not summon the residents of the house. Their home was protected by a high wall and locked gate. The way inside required ringing a bell outside the gate and waiting for the owner to come down and open it. I rang and rang the bell, but no one came. I was alone in a foreign country in the middle of the night, and I did not speak the language. For about 30 minutes ,there was no one to be seen whom I could speak to. Finally, I saw a man walking his dog, and I asked him for help and hoped he understood. He must have understood a little English, for he beckoned me to follow him. He took me to the entrance to the community, where there were two or three men who were like security guards. They telephoned the house repeatedly until someone finally answered, and he said he would meet me back at the house. By the time I got to my room, I was exhausted and slept fitfully until 10 a.m. the following morning.

I am indebted to this generous couple who fed me and took me on a sightseeing tour, as well as made me feel very much at home. It was a wonderful introduction to India and her hospitality. The next evening, my kind hosts took me to the train station to catch the night train to Haldwani. My senses were assaulted on the way to our destination. The traffic was chaotic, and there were many motorcycles, rickshaws, bicycles and other different forms of transportation. They all seemed to be going in many different directions, with almost all of them using their horns to pave the way. The train station was another new experience, as we had to pick our way through the platform because of the many homeless people who had camped down for the night. None of this was frightening or shocking, and in fact, I had the same sense of coming home. It all seemed quite familiar to me at a very deep level.

When the train arrived, it took some time to find my carriage, and when I did, I was momentarily stunned as I learned I was sharing a sleeping compartment with two Indian men. It took a while before I was able to sleep. I never slept deeply because I had some anxiety about missing the station where I had to get off, as well as some concern around the men, who turned out to be very gracious and helpful.

Arriving in Haldwani early in the morning, I had been told I would be met by Muniraji's driver. Muniraji was a merchant and family man from Haldwani and had become a constant companion to Babaji when Babaji was in His body. Babaji gave him more and more responsibility and according to the book 'I am Harmony', said "his work begins when I leave".[3] This was to become true when Muniraji assumed leadership of the Indian Ashram following Babaji's mahasamadi (death) in 1984. On that day, when I stepped out of the station, there must have been 50 men jostling around and asking me if I needed a ride. How was I to find my ride in this throng of taxi drivers? I held my head high and kept walking and saying no to all the men around me. The most persistent of the group then kept saying "Muniraji!" over and over, and I eventually realized he was the driver who had been sent to meet me. He took me to a hotel where I could shower and change, and it was another surprise when I saw the shower was a faucet halfway up the wall, with a bucket. After doing the best I could do to get clean, the driver then took me on to Muniraji's house, where there were other people gathered who were going on to the ashram. We spent a wonderful morning attending the sacred fire that Muniraji was conducting and eating a welcome breakfast of soup and bread and delicious-tasting sweet delicacies.

One of the most striking memories I have of India is that people were always showing up to help me. It was as if a guiding hand was gently orchestrating the entire trip and making sure I was well taken care of. I felt closer to Babaji during this time than at any other time in my life. I felt His presence in the people around me who suddenly appeared to help. I wanted to retain this feeling of being in the right place and people helping me when I returned to the United States. I had never felt it before, and I have never felt it as clearly since. I often use this memory as a model today when I start to think that things are not moving fast enough or happening the way I think they should happen.

After lunch with Muniraji and about 20 other people, a few of us were loaded into a van for our road trip to the ashram. I remember winding roads for most of the way and steep drops to the river below. The scenery was breathtaking, and I watched as we passed through beautiful landscaped terraces that seemed to be embedded in the side of lush green mountains. The river was almost dry in places, and I assumed we were following the path of the Ganges River. I experienced a kaleidoscope of contradictory thoughts throughout this trip that lasted a little more than two hours. This was everything I dreamed of, yet nothing compared to it; it was wonderful and different and touched me deeply in my sense of connection to the special land. I could hardly keep my eyes open as I was wracked with fatigue while at the same time I was vibrantly awake. It was definitely a collection of opposites.

Finally, we arrived at the ashram gates and were greeted by local lads who offered to carry in our bags. I was shown to a small room in which there were four single beds. There were about a dozen steps leading up to this room and a few dozen more that I had to negotiate to get to them. The first thing I noticed was how hard the bed was; it was just a wooden base with a thin pad covering the top. I wondered how I would ever be able to sleep on such a hard surface. Nothing had prepared me for that, and there was nothing in my luggage that would make it softer. I was advised of the daily schedule and left to my own devices.

I was still in a daze as I found my way to the temple for evening arati. I arrived early and found a seat against the inside wall. Sitting cross-legged on the floor, I watched all the activity around me. Imagine my surprise when suddenly something hit me very hard on the head! It almost drew tears to my eyes. I was stunned and had no idea what had happened. I wondered whether someone had thrown something at me, but I couldn't imagine why they would do that.

Looking all around me and seeing nothing unusual, I finally looked up and realized I was sitting directly under an electrical outlet. Further investigation revealed that the plug had jumped out of the outlet and hit me on the head. It was now lying at my side. I tried to make sense of this because I had never heard of plugs coming out of the wall suddenly and with that much force. There had to be a message here for me. Was Babaji trying to tell me something?

I was instantly reminded of one of Babaji's stories in which He was conducting a fire ceremony and suddenly picked up a piece of wood, thrust it in the fire and burned the arm of one of the men in the circle. This action caused great alarm by others who were present, and they questioned why He would do that. He replied, "I had to do that to settle his karma. Had I not done it, he would have had to live through something far worse," or words to that effect.

To this day, I often wonder why this happened and from what I was being protected. This was another example to me of how we cannot make sense of everything that happens to us or try to understand it, because we are looking from a mortal perspective and from our current life.

I quickly settled into the daily routine, which involved morning and evening arati and an early morning wakeup call at 4 a.m. indicating it was time to bathe and prepare for arati. Days were filled with karma yoga and daily fire ceremonies to celebrate the nine days of Navratri. This was all familiar to me because of all my visits to the Colorado ashram. What was not familiar was the physical layout of the Indian ashram and the number of stairs and steps that had to be climbed every day.

I had gone to Haidakhan thinking that I would be in a blissful state for most of the time and that it would be a time of great spiritual awareness. I was so wrong, and within a few days, I realized that it was a time of huge physical challenges. It involved more lessons on being mindful of my body, continuing the work that BodySoul had initiated.

The wakeup call was so early because all bathing took place in the Ganges. Preparing for the morning bath required gathering all necessary clothes, a flashlight and bathing items, and walking down 108 steep steps to the river. The only light available came from the stars and the moon, so it was quite an adventure finding the perfect spot in the river where I could bathe when the moon was hidden by clouds.

Since it was not the rainy season, the riverbed was low and most of the water suitable for bathing was close to the far bank. I had previously been coached on how to use a petticoat for the sake of modesty, so I had an idea of the logistics involved. I was not prepared for the coldness of the water, and it took my breath away and reminded me of swimming lessons in high school where the water was never more than 60 degrees, even in the middle of summer. The cold water was a shock to my system but left me feeling invigorated and alive. After the first morning bath, I began to enjoy these quiet mornings. The riverbed was full of rocks of all shapes and sizes, and they became my friends. I was no longer scared when they loomed up before me in the darkness and I began to recognize each one. It was as if I were forming a personal relationship with each of them. One became the guardian of my clothes as I took my bath, while another provided a rounded seat where I could sit and rest; still others led the way to my favorite spot in the river. For me, they often took the form of birds or animals and I felt they were there to support me. They spoke to me and represented continuity and age. Most of them had been there for eons. I was aware that Babaji Himself had trodden on many of these stones and was guarded by these rocks as He bathed in the river. It was really an amazing experience.

The walk up the 108 steps was something else! I learned quickly that I also had to negotiate these steps one or two times more every day. The ashram was built on either side of the Ganges and all the fire ceremonies, as well as lunch, were held on the opposite side of the river. Over the course of the first few days, it became increasingly difficult for me to make the journey from one side of the river to the other. By the time I had climbed the 108 steps, I was pretty well wiped out. After a few days, I could barely walk. My entire body was aching and sore from the steps, as well as the hard bed. I was miserable and reduced to walking very slowly and deliberately, and calculating how I could get from A to B with as few steps as possible.

It was a lesson in mindfulness, as I had to pay attention to every detail of my physical life. I was scared for any lapse in concentration that might cause excruciating pain. My mind was crowded with overwhelming thoughts that I had been carrying my entire life: *I am not good enough...Life is a struggle...This is so hard*...and many more. I also began to fall, as it required enormous effort to put one foot in front of the other. My balance was off, and my body was like a quivering mass of jelly while my mind was a quivering mass of anxiety, judgment and negativity. I was worrying about falling again and not being able to keep up with the necessary karma yoga and daily activities. To put it bluntly, I was a mess. Someone finally suggested I go down to the hospital that was on the grounds and talk with them. I was not aware that this hospital was open to the public, and it was a relief to finally be able to ask for help.

The hospital visit was an adventure in itself. I was given some medication and advised to come back at 3 p.m. for a massage that would help my sore body. The massage I received was like no massage I had ever experienced before. As I sat naked on a massage table, warm oil was poured on the top of my head and massaged down my entire body. This was followed by sitting in a steam box for 10 minutes and then a 30-minute relaxation when I was left alone to lie down in comfort. A cool shower was the conclusion to this strange massage. Returning to my room, I lay on the bed and fell into a deep sleep, where I stayed until the 4 a.m. wakeup call. The next day, all my physical pain and discomfort was gone and never reappeared for the rest of the trip.

Two days later, I had to return one more time to the hospital, having contracted some form of dysentery. I had been careful to watch what I was eating and mostly just ate at the lunchtime bhandara (feast). One day, I decided not to go across the river for lunch, so I stopped at the chai shop that was situated on the steps leading down to the river. Obviously, I ate something that did not agree with my stomach and became violently ill. It's one thing having this problem when you are in your own home, but it's completely different when you have only five outdoor toilets that serve dozens of people and where you often have to stand in line.

Fortunately, after some exploration, I discovered a more private washroom that was in a building close by. Having been given different medication by the hospital, I was able to recover in a couple of days. Since I could not eat during that time, I emerged on the third day like a newborn baby. I was very lightheaded and felt as weak as a kitten. It was as if my body had been emptied and readjusted. and I was leaving with a newness I could not explain. I had, in effect, been reborn for the second time in my life.

It was now nearing the end of my trip, and it was as if I had lived three lifetimes in nine days. I had lost all sense of time, and it was somewhat confusing. It was not all a difficult and challenging time. My favorite time of the day was early in the morning when Babaji's kutir (room) was open for chandan. Chandan is a daily ritual that takes place early in the morning following bathing and before arati. Sandalwood paste, Kumkum (a red decorative powder) and rice are placed in sequence on the third eye or swiped across the forehead to symbolize the presence of Divine energy. Sandalwood is used to cool the mind, and rice symbolizes the purity of the soul.

Babaji's room was very small, with just space enough to house a single bed and very few people. It was located on a small patio that overlooked the Ganges and had an amazing view down the river. In the center of the patio was a huge peepal tree whose enormous branches offered shade to all the visitors. I loved to visit this patio, where Babaji's presence was the most palpable to me. I could imagine Him spending time on this patio and sitting under the tree, surrounded by His followers. This energy was also present in His room, so going for morning chandan was like a personal visit to Babaji Himself.

Since the room could only hold two or three people at a time, visitors would line up to receive their chandan, and the line would often extend out to the patio. I was always reminded of the Episcopal and Catholic communion services, where people would surge toward the front of the church where communion was being offered. It was a special time and made more special by the fact that it was taking place in Babaji's room, where He had slept and spent a great deal of His time.

One morning, as I stood on the threshold of His room, I silently asked, "Please, Baba, come into my heart."

Immediately, I felt huge waves of energy pulsating through my entire body. I knew that He was there, and He had heard me.

Darshan with Shri Muniraji was another memorable time. I was holding this intense desire to meet with him at some point while I was there. Finally, after arati one morning, there was an announcement that someone was taking appointments for these meetings. Immediately, my mind kicked in with a litany of familiar thoughts: *How do I get what I want? I will never be able to find a way to make this happen! I don't know how to go about finding the person who is setting the appointments.* And so on.

I was literally feeling sick to my stomach from the stress of these thoughts. Finally, I was reminded of Shdema Goodman's book, *Babaji, Meeting with Truth*. She describes numerous instances where Baba threw her out of the ashram, which caused her to become introspective and explore the thoughts that may have led to his decisions. She said that as soon as she righted the thought, He would immediately show up and tell her she could come back.

I was able to drop these troublesome thoughts, and when I did, someone approached me and said my appointment was to be at 4 p.m. that day and I would be with 16 other people. It is always amazing to me how simple and free-flowing life can be and how difficult I can make it for myself. India taught me this. If we remain open and receptive, life flows in a free, natural and unfettered manner. As soon as we have negative thoughts or operate from unconscious negative beliefs, life becomes more difficult. It's as if the energy coming from God is like a clear, young stream. Every negative thought is a pebble or a rock that we throw in the stream, causing the water to slow down, or worse still, dam up so we no longer have access to this life-giving energy.

Sitting with Muniraji that afternoon allowed me to be in his presence and watch his interaction with each person in the group. He exuded kindness and a profound humility. It seemed interminable before it was my turn to talk to him and I asked him one question that I had been struggling with: "How do I tell the difference between my will and Babaji's will for me?"

He responded quickly and simply, saying, "Do your sadhana every day and you will be okay." Sadhana is a daily spiritual practice, so he was telling me to do my daily practice and things would take care of themselves. Since that time, I have followed his advice, and every time I run into a situation where I question what I should do, I remember Muniraji's words and just trust in Babaji.

Muniraji gave me an Indian name that day, and in many ways I felt I had been baptized by him. The name he gave me is Ila (pronounced *Eela*), which means "earth" or "speech" in Sanskrit. It seems significant to me that it should translate to "earth," because I was led to Babaji initially by an astrologer who said I had no earth signs in my astrological chart and needed help with breathing. Maybe with this new name, I had somehow found the grounding that appeared to be missing in my chart.

The end of my stay at Haidakhan was approaching all too quickly, and I wanted to absorb all the sights and sounds and energy that surrounded me every day so I could take them home with me. I would stand against the wall outside Babaji's kutir and gaze down the Ganges and feast my eyes on the surrounding mountains and terraced hillsides. I would relish evening arati, the bustle, the noise, the cacophony of colors and sound and the singing and dancing. I would walk more slowly down the 108 steps and across the river, realizing that my feet were walking where Babaji's once stepped. I was particularly intrigued by the people who were living on the riverbed. They had built small one-room houses from the stones in the river. They would sleep in these structures, which would also provide protection from the elements. Many would set up tables outside, from which they would sell food and drinks. They would build a smaller structure next to where they slept, and I assumed this was used as a toilet. They were entirely self-sufficient, living a remarkably simple life in harmony with the river and its surroundings.

I asked about the lives of these people and was told they would arrive during the dry season when the river had dried up considerably. They would then build their quarters and leave before the monsoon season started. Once the rains came, all the buildings were washed away and the rocks would fall back to the riverbed. I was struck by how much this illustrated the idea of impermanence and how they lived on the Earth with a minimal footprint. The concept of impermanence is central to Buddhist teachings that everything is fleeting and pain is caused by grasping or not being able to accept this fact. It was liberating for me to know that the tradesmen who were living on the riverbed were actively practicing and living a life of impermanence.

The last day of my stay arrived, and I was sad to be leaving. It seemed as if I had lived many lifetimes in this short period. I packed my belongings early so I would have the rest of the morning to attend the final celebrations before I was to leave at 3 p.m. Returning to my room after lunch, I was stopped cold in my tracks. On my bed sat Babaji; it looked as if he had been waiting for me. Once again, I had that old, now-familiar feeling of goosebumps that reminded me of the recognition of the meeting of Human and Divine. I blinked, and when my eyes opened again, I saw that it was not really Babaji but a framed picture of Him that had somehow appeared on my bed. I had not seen that particular picture before and could not believe that my initial reaction had felt like I was seeing Him in form. This was an enormous gift to me and a reminder that He would be with me on my travels home and through the rest of my life. After some questioning, I eventually learned that my roommate had found this picture and thought I might like to take it home. It now sits in the place of honor on my home altar and is always a reminder of Babaji and my trip to India.

Another guide showed up just before I was due to leave, in the form of an older woman who had been staying at the ashram and was now returning home to her family. She was to travel with me to the train station and wait with me to ensure I caught the correct train that would take me back to Delhi. We spent a relaxing afternoon camped out in the station waiting room, eating snacks she had brought with her and taking occasional naps. The rest of my trip was uneventful as I stayed in Delhi with the same couple for one night before leaving for home.

I received many spiritual lessons from my trip to Haidakhan, and I think in many ways I was torn down and reassembled, both physically and emotionally. It is impossible for me to know exactly what happened on that trip, but there are a few gifts I traveled home with that I treasure.

India provided me with a model for simplicity and impermanence. The people I met were eager to help. They lived simply and accepted the impermanence of their lives. They seemed happy and content. I loved the seeming chaos of India and the realization that there was order in the chaos and vibrancy of their daily living. I know that this trip helped me trust more and have more faith. It was as if India were a crucible in which all the challenges of daily living showed up regularly and I was acutely aware of my reaction to them. I learned to know my distorted and negative thoughts more intimately and to see the impact they had on my body. I also saw the futility of them and how easy it was to change them. I especially learned that God, or Babaji, was always beside me and orchestrating my surroundings so that life was easier for me if I allowed it to be that way. I learned to not trust my expectations, because I never would have imagined that this trip would focus so much on my body. By not putting emphasis on expectations, I learned to live more fully in the present and to accept what is.

A major lesson was to become clearer about the importance of our physical bodies. I have had this reminder so often in my lifetime. On the one hand, it will eventually degrade and die, but on the other hand, if our body is hurting or sick, we are unable to fully and enthusiastically carry out our service. The body is our vehicle through life and we can care for it intimately, which means we will get many miles of trustworthy service, or we can disregard its need for regular checkups and oil changes, meaning it will be less reliable and susceptible to unexpected breakdowns. We are solely responsible for its care, and without it running smoothly, the rest of our lives will suffer.

Being in Haidakhan and so closely connected to Babaji, helped me understand that dreams really can come true and innermost desires can be materialized. Ultimately, I understood the importance of daily sadhana, gratitude and focus on God.

It was only 12 years ago that I took this trip to Haidakhan. It had taken me almost a lifetime to make it, because I was too scared to believe in my dreams and take steps toward achieving them. God can only do so much for us, but ultimately, we must take action to fully live our lives, work toward our goals, and trust Him to support us.

I have learned that the inner path can only take us so far, but to be truly happy in human form, we have to take chances in the outside world, since it is the dance between both of these worlds that helps us feel complete.

The outside world will reflect our inner world, and any changes we make inwardly will take a while to be seen outside of ourselves. When I left India, I knew I had changed, but I could not explain how.

Now, when I look back, I can see some of the changes more clearly. My trust in God has deepened and my poverty consciousness has healed. Eleven years ago, my husband and I were living a meager existence in a small two-bedroom apartment and were paying off a sizeable debt. It was the second time we had almost faced bankruptcy, the first being before Babaji came into my life. It took us three or years of living within a strict budget before we paid off all our debt. Within two months of doing this, my dad passed away, leaving us an inheritance that allowed us to buy a small home and live comfortably. I did not miss the irony of this. I had always seen my dad as overly cautious with his money. His early comment, "You are only as good as your earning power," had resulted in my failing to recognize the importance of having a financial situation that provides for basic human needs. I realized that paying off the debt and then receiving the gift from Dad was a major life lesson that he had provided for me. My complex around money had finally been healed.

Since then, I have learned that the universe provides for me if I do my part. My anxiety has lessened as I have learned to trust myself and others more. I am living a simpler life within my means and have no desire to add more material goods. I set up an altar in my new home and offer daily prayers of gratitude to Babaji and the Divine Mother and take the time to read motivational words every day. I no longer feel the need to prove anything, and I realize now that I was always pushing myself to the extreme as I tried to "be somebody" in the world.

I guess you can say I have finally learned who I am, and I am happy with that. I learned from the tradesmen in the riverbed in India that everything is fleeting, and I try to appreciate my life and everything around me. I also work hard at not projecting fears into the future concerning what may happen. I am a calmer, more easygoing person who is more comfortable in her own skin.

This has all had a ripple effect on my clients, who continue to call and arrive at my office, even though I spend no money on advertising. More and more frequently, these are people who are committed to understanding themselves and finding and following their own inner paths. Without any doubts, I can tell them, "Your dreams really can come true."

Notes

[1] Arnold Toynbee, Reddit, last accessed February 13,2021, (Toynbee n.d.) reddit.com/r/aznidentity/comments/kmslyu/this_quote_sums_up_ western_civilization_barbarism

[2] Marion Woodman. *The Ravaged Bridegroom—Masculinity in Women*, Inner City Books, p. 211.

[3] Radhe Shyam, *I am Harmony*, p. 231.

Personal Thoughts

Even when you think you have your life all mapped out, things happen that shape your destiny in ways you might never have imagined.[1]

—Deepak Chopra

17.

ARE YOU ON THE RIGHT PATH?

Do you believe you have a destiny, or do you think your life is based on pure chance? What is the difference between destiny and fate? Why do you think you are here at this time and in this body? How do you know when you are following your destiny and on the right path? These are all important questions—and the older we get, the more important they seem to be.

I obviously believe that I am living my destiny because of the miracles I have lived. I could never have imagined my future when I was a teenager or young adult, and I can barely believe the things that have happened to me over the past 50 years. It was not something I chose, but rather, something that chose me, and that I was thankfully open to exploring. My life experience has given me some insight into how I knew, and still know, that I am where I am meant to be.

When I was trying to decide whether to move from Memphis to Florida, I was agonizing over whether this decision was being made solely by my ego or whether I was being guided by Babaji. I felt absolutely stuck and was getting no answers and no guidance about the decision. I happened to be in Canada to attend one of Marion's workshops when I met one of the women from the group and we decided to go out for breakfast. I was talking to her about my dilemma and posed the question to her: "How do we know when we are being guided by God or the ego?"

As I talked to her about this possible move, I started to cry. The tears just sprang out of my eyes with no thought. The emotion touched me when I was explaining to her the incidents that led us to explore this option for our future. I was surprised by my reaction, and I will never forget her response. She leaned back in her chair, looked at me and said, "Duh!" It's as if she were saying, "There's your answer, and you do know."

Her recognition that this possible move touched such a deep place in me resonated with my soul, and it was at that point it became clear. I knew we had to move to Florida, and the direction was coming from Spirit .

So, what is the difference between destiny and fate? This recently became clear to me while watching an excellent documentary entitled "Daughters of Destiny". It relates the story of a successful Indian businessman living in the USA who decided to open a special school for children in India. The concept was to take children at four years of age, from their homes in the lowest caste of society and enroll them in a boarding school where they received an excellent academic education, as well as a re-culturalization. They were treated with dignity and respect and held to high moral and academic standards. These children grew up into successful young adults who went to college and were able to provide much needed help and support to their families and communities. This extraordinary man who pioneered this idea, said that the young women in the documentary were born into 'the untouchable caste' which was their fate. Their destiny was to become successful in the outside world and ultimately to help transform their communities. Fate then is an inevitable course of events, but destiny is the ability to change these events for the better.

Once we are living our destiny, there are certain signs along the way that indicate that we are following this special path. It frequently feels like a conversation with a Divine guidance. I have outlined below in bold, a selection of the signs that have been frequent in my life.

Verbalizing our inner conflict helps us find answers. The question becomes more real when it is validated by another person. Also, depending on the listener, we may be asked relevant questions that help us find the answer. Psychotherapy was an important stage for me because I was mirrored and supported, and it led to a profession I love.

Emotional response is a good hint that we are being touched at a deep level, and it can bring about **an "aha" moment**. This is an immediate knowing that automatically comes from the body and not from the head. I have never liked the idea of making an important decision by listing all the pluses and minuses and then making the decision based on the most pluses. It sounds good, but it is usually the head that makes the decision and not the body or the heart. You may have had the experience of writing such a list that is full of negatives, and yet you know in your gut it is something you want to do or must do.

Listening to our gut feeling or intuition is paramount to walking our destiny. If we are not grounded in our bodies, we are not able to do this. For me, Marion's workshops were instrumental in helping me learn to recognize and trust my intuition or gut feelings.

Synchronicities are also good signposts on our spiritual path. Carl Jung spoke frequently about synchronicity and described it as "the simultaneous occurrence of two meaningfully but not causally connected events."[2] He says there is a relationship between the two events that is an energetic relationship but that does not follow the normal transmission of energy. He uses an example of discussing a dream with a client in which she had been given a golden scarab. While she was describing the dream, he heard a noise at the window behind him, which sounded like a gentle tapping. He turned around and saw a flying insect at the window. Upon opening the window, the insect flew inside and he discovered it was a scarab beetle—an insect that was not native to Switzerland, where this took place.[3]

These special moments signal an alignment between our words or actions and the energy around us. They are brief periods in which everything seems to come together as they work toward a certain completeness or wholeness.

There have been a variety of synchronistic events in my life—the first and biggest one being when the astrologer told me I was susceptible to breathing problems many years ago, after I had been seeing doctors for this very symptom. This is what led me to Christina and ultimately to Babaji.

There are two more of these events that were very vivid, and both involved Babaji and my spiritual path. However, synchronicities can happen to anyone at any time and should not be disregarded. It can be as simple as two friends picking up the phone to call each other at the same time.

During the early days of my initial meeting with Babaji and the rebirthing session that literally changed my life, I went to London at the same time as Christina. She was lecturing at the Body Mind Spirit show in London, and I was vacationing with my mother and her friend. I am not sure of the details, since it happened about 30 years ago. I am sure about the synchronicities that took place during the trip.

I spent a good deal of time on the exhibition floor of the show. Many people had set up booths to sell their goods and services, which all related to health, healing and spirituality. I was especially drawn to a small booth where a woman was giving some kind of foot treatment. I later learned it was called the Metamorphic Technique. I was drawn instinctively to the lively personality of the woman who was doing the practice. I was also drawn to the practice but told myself that it was something I could never do: allow another person to work on my feet. I think it was a decision based on the fact that Christ used to have his feet washed by his disciples. This made me feel very undeserving or unworthy.

I spoke briefly to the practitioner and then went on my way to check out other booths. Over the course of the next hour, I would keep bumping into her on the floor and she would keep urging me to get my feet done. I finally surrendered and said I would. We struck up an immediate friendship and connection, and as I sat with my feet in her lap in this tiny booth, we talked and laughed as if we had known each other our entire lives.

By the end of the session, she had invited me to go to her home in Surrey to spend the night. Since I was returning to the U.S. the next day, she said she would take me to the airport for my flight. I agreed, which was extremely unusual behavior for me, since I tend to be thoughtful and deliberate in making decisions. I called my mother to tell her I would meet her at the gate the following day, and I was faced with a barrage of questions: "Who is this woman? Where does she live? You are staying the night with someone you don't even know?"

I assured her that I would be fine, and Siobhan and I set off in her car to Surrey.

I began to doubt my decision as we took this drive and she told me that we had been invited to a garden party that night. She assured me we would not make it a late night.

When we arrived at her home, I was astounded. It was like walking into my own home. She had the same pictures on the walls and the same books on the bookshelf. We were definitely twin souls in that we had an immediate connection physically, emotionally and spiritually.

I went off to the garden party with some resistance. Had I known we would do this, I think I would have declined the invitation to go home with her. We arrived, and she placed a drink in my hand and introduced me to a male friend of hers. As he and I chatted, he asked me what had brought me over to London, and I explained that I was on vacation and had attended the Body Mind Spirit exhibition. He responded, "I am not going this year, and there is only one person who I would have wanted to meet." To my utmost shock, he mentioned Christina's name.

I immediately felt I was in a time warp. I was thousands of miles from my home in Memphis and in an entirely different country, and I had walked into a house that was like mine on the inside and met a chap who wanted to meet Christina. The synchronicity left me a little disoriented and with a sense of another energetic dimension.

As I mentioned before, my parents were not very accepting of me and the decisions I made after my initial rebirth. They feared I was getting drawn into a cult, and they were concerned for me. Over the years, it became less of an issue, especially when they saw that nothing would stop me. They also saw that I was happier and had not left behind all my possessions to go and live in another state. I knew this was my spiritual path moving forward, and it became the priority in my life.

Many years later, my parents went to visit family in California. I spoke to my mother by phone while she was there, and she told me they had been to this wonderful place of beauty and calmness in Encinitas. She said they had bought a book for me they thought I might like. I had an idea of what was coming, and when they returned, I was thrilled when she proudly presented me with a hard copy of *Autobiography of a Yogi*, by Paramahansa Yogananda. It was as if we went full circle from their fears of a cult to them accepting me and picking out Yogananda's book as a gift. I am sure Babaji had something to do with their choice of book.

Experiencing strange happenings is an indication that we are being guided and are not in control of our lives. While I was working with Christina, I attended a workshop she led, which culminated in a fire-walking experience. I received permission from my husband's friend to use his home and the land on his farm for the purposes of the workshop. It was a full day, and we ended the day gathering in the house for snacks and personal sharing of the fire walk. Before long, we heard a dog barking at the door. One participant went to the door and saw a mangy dog that was obviously hungry and homeless. She immediately felt sorry for the dog and took it some food. This started an hour-long lila (play or drama) about whether we should be feeding the dog or leaving it to go away to find food for itself. The argument became quite heated, and the group quickly divided into two camps. One camp felt that feeding the dog would only create dependency and the dog would always be hanging around this home. The second camp believed the dog could take care of itself, as it obviously had been doing, and that feeding it wouldn't change that. I seemed to be the observer and watched, fascinated as the energy grew and everyone was focused on the dog. The evening finally ended, and we all went our separate ways.

The next morning, I received a phone call from my friend who had answered the door and became the leading advocate for the dog. She recounted that she was the last to leave the night before and had decided to take the dog home with her.

She piled him into the back seat of her car, and off they went. She said she had intended to feed him, clean him up and give him a home. Talking with her husband, they decided to put him out on their small patio overnight so they could clean him in the morning. After she got up, she went to the patio to feed him and he was nowhere to be seen. He had disappeared from a small patio that was surrounded by a 10-foot wall. We both knew immediately that Babaji was talking to us through that dog.

Another incident that attracted my attention and told me that Babaji was present occurred when my father died.

It was 5 a.m. on the morning of February 14, 2013. I received an urgent telephone call from the head nurse at the residence where Dad was living. She did not tell me anything except, "get over here immediately." My husband and I rapidly dressed ourselves and drove as fast as we could to answer this call. We knew instinctively that Dad had passed away. He was 91 years old and was declining and losing weight. He was a little forgetful but was still able to get up every day and go downstairs for his meals and to spend the day in his favorite chair. Sometimes, an outside aide who had become a valued friend would take him out for lunch. In fact, he had gone to the art gallery and lunch the previous day and I had left him the night before, watching a movie downstairs. I would never have known that death was imminent, and he didn't seem to be in any pain.

When we arrived that morning, the nurse told us that the aide had woken him up early as usual, and he had asked for water. She took him some water and told him she would be back soon to help him get up and get dressed. When she returned 30 minutes later, he had passed away. The staff did everything they could to deter us from entering his room to say our last goodbyes before he was to be picked up. I insisted and knew it would be the closure I needed as we moved forward. Tom and I spent about five or ten minutes with him, and then we returned to the hallway, where there was a police officer and an elderly lady sitting in the chair outside the room. I recognized her as a woman who had previously sat with us for meals and knew she was also someone that the staff teased Dad about. It seemed they had formed a close friendship, but I had never been introduced to her.

She looked up at me and said, "Your dad sent me to talk to you and tell you how much he loved you." It's difficult to describe the impact these words had on me. It was as if they came from an angel. My dad had never told me he loved me; in fact, I had been questioning this, as he became quieter and less friendly in recent months. I went to give her a hug and then unexpectedly collapsed on her lap and sobbed into her comforting shoulders. This was the first time I had felt any grief or sadness since hearing the news of his passing. It must have been quite a sight for the onlookers watching a 65+ year old lady crying in the lap of an 80+ senior. After a while I recovered enough to ask her name and what unit she lived in. I was astounded when she said, "I'm in room 108."

The number 108 is sacred in Eastern religions, and all the malas have 108 beads. It is a number I have encountered frequently in my spiritual community. When I heard this woman say her room number, I knew immediately that Babaji was behind this visit from my dad's friend. It was as if Babaji had sent her to tell me of His love for me, which provided some comfort at this sad time.

It was only when I arrived home a few hours later that I realized Dad had died on the date of Babaji's Mahasamadhi. This is when the soul of a saint consciously departs from His/Her body. I was thinking about this special coincidence all that day. Babaji was very present with me and a constant reminder that He was in charge and was taking good care of me and my father.

Albert Kreinheder, in his book *Body and Soul*, talks about the phenomenon of **goosebumps**. He writes: "Plato has said that whenever anyone has an experience of original beauty (an archetypal experience), it causes the feathers to sprout. As he explained, in the olden days, the soul was known to be feathered, and the goosebumps that arise on the skin are the sprouting of the feathers of the soul." He goes on to say that it represents a meeting of the "sacred and the profane" and is both a "psychic and a physical experience."[4]

Over the years, I have found this to be true, and having learned to trust the feathers, I always know when I am on the right track. They often accompany a synchronistic event. Today, when I sit with a client, goosebumps frequently validate something I may say. I am aware of the presence of the Divine in that moment.

Signs and symbols are not always available, and we can spend months and years with a silence that is thunderous to the ears as we wander in barren deserts. Our faith is tested as we wonder if we have been living under an illusion and whether this is all a figment of our imagination. At those times, it has been crucial to have a community of faith so we can be supported by like-minded people. For me, it has been my Babaji community and ashram home. They always uplift my spirit and help to keep Him alive in my heart when it seems I am all alone. For others,it may be a yoga community, an environmental group, a church or a synagogue.

Wise teachers and guides have shown up in my life to support and validate me from one step to the next, and I am sincerely grateful to them. Sometimes it is a perilous journey to place trust in an elder or teacher, and we do not always learn lessons the way we think we should. For me, it has been a process of learning to love and trust in myself. In the beginning, I realized I was looking for the mother I never had and would want teachers to be this mother. I slowly learned I had to trust myself, with no expectations of anyone else. It was a difficult lesson.

To summarize, if we are open and listen with our heart and see with our inner eye, we know we are on the right path by certain signs, our dreams and the fulfillment we feel inside. This does not mean we do not face enormous challenges that can be painful and confusing. It does mean that if we have a solid center and faith in the journey, these difficulties will be easier to handle. It is important to remember we are being pulled by something greater than us, and as Carl Jung said, we are always moving toward wholeness.

Notes

[1] Deepak Chopra, Goodreads, last accessed February 13, 2021, goodreads.com/quotes/93256, (Chopra n.d.)

[2] C.G. Jung, CW vol 8, *The Structure and Dynamics of the Psyche*, p. 441.

[3] Ibid., p. 438.

[4] Albert Kreinheder, Inner City Books, *Body and Soul*, p. 28.

Personal Thoughts

PART 6

BRINGING HOME THE TREASURE

At the beginning, the Guru is God; it is as if the human being embraces tightly the idea of the Guru as being everything, but little by little the Guru disentangles himself from the embrace, so to say, and points to God. . . [1]

—From *Daughter of Fire*, by Irina Tweedie

18

THE ULTIMATE GIFT

I struggled for months to find an adequate ending to my story—and there was nothing...nothing at all. I was a deep, dry well. I told myself that maybe it was because I am still living my life, so the end has not yet been written. It took the sickness of my husband and ultimately his passing, followed by four months of mourning, before the clouds lifted and I was able to pick up the pen once more.

We had spent eight weeks in three different hospitals trying to discover the source and treatment for a blood problem Tom was experiencing. During that time, we never once gave up hope that he would recover and come home. When he was down, I lifted his spirits—and when I was exhausted and less sure, he lifted mine. We focused on creating as much normalcy as we could under the conditions as our lives centered around daily blood counts and various medications and procedures. There were many happy times as we watched football and basketball games together on TV and shared breakfast together daily after meeting with the doctor.

At one hospital, we had visits from one of our favorite nurses, who would pop in and see us on her way to work or as she was leaving. These moments were precious and became more special as time went on. He was finally stabilized and sent home on Thanksgiving Day with plans to set up outpatient treatment close to home. Although we arrived home with no food and no stores open to buy any, we were happy to be home and spent the next couple days trying to pick up the pieces of our old life.

An unexpected visit by distant friends surprised and delighted us on Saturday, and we had an enjoyable evening. This all changed on Sunday when the doctor called to say we had to return to the ER because of another low blood count. To cut a long story short, he was admitted to the third hospital at this point, and once more, rounds of the same tests and treatments began with staff who were not considerate of our frustration and didn't seem to care about our experience over the previous seven weeks.

By now, I was angry with the staff of this hospital and especially angry with Babaji. How could He be leaving us alone to cope with this situation? I had been praying to Him for almost eight weeks, and there was absolutely no response. How is it He could send me dreams and messages when my parents were sick and at the end of their lives and He seemed to be ignoring us now?

We were floundering in deep waters, and He was nowhere to be seen. He was not listening to my pleas for guidance, and He was not coming to me in my dreams. I was beginning to feel exhausted and confused. I questioned myself: *Have I been following a figment of my imagination all my life? Have I put supreme faith in Babaji when He doesn't even exist? Has my entire life been a lie?* The questions would not go away, and I had no answers. My faith was sorely being tested, and I had nowhere else to turn.

Finally, on Wednesday, I managed to stop the rapid rounds of duplicate tests and treatments and found a doctor who would listen. My husband was transferred to hospice that night.

Early Friday morning and after a particularly restless night for Tom, the staff talked me into going home. They said I needed to eat, rest and take a shower and I would feel better. I took their advice, collapsed on our bed and awoke three hours later from the following dream:

I am watching from the bank, as a woman is pulling Marion (Woodman) in a rubber dinghy down some rapids. They are being tossed around and the dinghy is flying from one side of the river to the other. Both women are laughing and seem to be enjoying themselves. I am horrified and shout to the woman to stop. I say, "Do you not realize she is old and frail, and this is too dangerous" I wake up with Marion's words ringing in my ears: "This is my life and my death, and I will do them how I please."[2]

The reality of our situation hit me with a force that reduced me to rubble. In that instant, I knew this was telling me it was time to let go of Tom and he had to live out his destiny in his own way. The grief exploded with a force I could never have imagined.

I returned to hospice and arrived about 12 noon. Tom passed away within ten minutes of my arrival.

The nurse generously offered to let me spend some time with him, so I sat next to him, battle-weary and overwhelmed with emotion. This turned out to be one of the momentous times of my life. I could barely take my eyes off him and could hardly believe how peaceful he looked. It was such a contrast from the past few nights, when he had been restless and distressed. He looked so happy, and I asked myself, "Is this what death looks like?"

It felt like one of the most natural states in the world, and for some reason, I was surprised. I felt relief that he was no longer in distress, but my heart was ripped open as I realized this was the last hour I had to spend with him on the physical plane. I was overcome with grief that flowed over and through me in waves. In the midst of it all, I heard the words, "We taught each other how to love."

Did they come from Tom? God? They resonated so deeply with me, and another paroxysm of grief overtook me like a tidal wave. I allowed myself to ride the wave, and I was finally washed up on a distant shore as I gazed out of the window in front of me and contemplated those words.

I realized the absolute truth of this, and my heart was touched once more and filled with gratitude and recognition of the enormity of this gift of love. Neither one of us felt genuinely loved as children—and yet, somehow, we had found each other and traversed 45 years of challenges and happiness, pain and friendship. Through it all, we had learned how to truly love each other. We had learned to be authentic with ourselves and each other, and we were now able to demonstrate this love and concern. Our love for the other was almost greater than our love for ourselves. Sometimes, this was a fine balancing act, and we would struggle to find a place where we were still true to ourselves while also being there for the other.

The silence deepened, and I found myself wrapped in a cocoon of ultimate peace. There were no words for it. It was beyond anything I had ever felt—except, perhaps, for the rebirthing experience that changed my life so many years ago. It was as if a magical, profound spell had been cast around us, and I never wanted it to end.

I have thought about this experience many times since. Something in me changed as a result of it. It shattered my heart and I discovered within it a deep well of peace, love and vulnerability. I have spent my entire life searching for something that was enigmatic. I have traveled to, and lived in, three different countries in my quest—and almost overnight, I realized it was love I had been searching for all along. The ultimate irony was that it took the loss of the person who had shown it to me and taught me its ways to create this realization. It was human love at its worst and at its best.

The Divine love came from Babaji, yet I now understand I had carried Babaji in my heart in the image of a human being. He was the Babaji I see in pictures and on the Internet. When I thought of him, I saw this form and heard his words. It was a child's simple understanding of Christ and the Divine.

The tsunami in my heart broke this image into a thousand pieces, and now I was seeing Him everywhere I looked, but in a different form. He was in the special times Tom and I shared with family, friends and staff while he was in the hospital. He was in the pervasive peace that enveloped us in the hospice room. He was in the love shown by treasured friends who brought food and comfort at a difficult time. He was in the early morning bird song and the Sun that peeked its head above the horizon every day, bringing with it a tapestry of colors. He was in the beauty of the sky at sunset. Suddenly, He was everywhere I looked.

Intellectually, I had known this to be the case, but it took a devastating loss to help me feel it, see it and know it in the deep recesses of my heart and soul.

I knew I had been looking for this all along, and I understood it had not been caused by the loss of my love, but rather, by the expansion of my love into a much vaster comprehension of God and guru. It was the realization that Love is everywhere, which is ultimately what my life had been teaching me.

Almost 40 years ago in the foothills of the Kumaon hills in northeast India, a charismatic and prophetic teacher passed away on Valentine's Day. He had been hinting about His death for some time, telling the people around Him that He would soon be going on a long trip which He would have to take alone. When it happened, He went quickly and peacefully, causing shock waves to cascade through the immediate community, as well as through the rest of the world, where others who knew Him and loved Him were living.

The day before He passed, for the last time, He talked about the coming radical world changes when he said, "Destruction has to happen for two reasons—because people still think of only 'I' and 'mine'; this is not the truth, not the spiritual way, not love; and because everyone wants to be big and no one wants to be small. . . . Therefore it is irreversible".3

As a human being, He said His heart was breaking because He was "bearing the pain of the entire Universe." The following day, He was to die of a heart attack.

His mortal death caused heartbreak for hundreds and thousands of people who had found their way to His feet and into His heart. They could not believe or accept that He was gone from them.

For a few days following His death, it was as if the earth stopped breathing. There was no wind, and it was said that the birds stopped singing and the skies were cloudy and overcast. There was an impenetrable silence. Even the sun stayed hidden from view behind the clouds as the entire cosmos mourned the loss of this Divine Being in human form.

What the world was unable to see was that at the moment His heart burst, a meteor shower of Divine love and energy was expelled throughout the world, carrying sparks of this light and love into the hearts of those who loved Him, as well as those whose hearts were open. This was to create a world-wide web of love, protection and guidance that would support others through the catastrophic changes that would become apparent in the next century.

This special guru or teacher was known as Haidakhan Babaji. In His new form, He continues to connect with others heart to heart through dreams, visions and visits to the numerous centers that have been established for Him across the globe.

Notes

[1] Irina Tweedie, *Daughter of Fire*, p. 338.

[2] Marion Woodman. *Marion Woodman Foundation BodySoul Rhythms® Leadership Training Workshops*

[3] Gertude Reichel, editor, *Babaji—The Unfathomable*. s.l. p. 154

Personal Thoughts

19.
POSTSCRIPT

I have just returned home from my morning walk and have been enjoying my daily cup of coffee. It is now almost seven months since I lost Tom. During this time, collectively, we have faced the ravages of COVID-19 and many other social problems. I have personally faced loneliness, grief and vulnerability.

I am realizing more each day that when Tom passed away, he was born into a new world as he left this one. In the same way, I feel that his death initiated a birthing for me. It is one I didn't ask for and didn't want, but I find myself standing on the cusp of something new. I am approaching the threshold of a new life.

I am not sure if this means I am close to a physical or a symbolic death, as I prepare, at some level, to embrace this new beginning. Either way, I am comforted in the knowledge that Babaji is with me and God reveals Herself to me daily in my dreams, in the faces of people around me, in the flowers that turn their petals toward the sun and in the Earth's bounty. I am inspired and calmed by Her presence. (Notice how I now refer to God as *She*, for throughout this process, I have come to learn more about, and love, the feminine face of God. Along my travels, I have discovered Her in myself, as well as in the world around me.)

Today is a little different from other mornings as I reflect on the treasure I am carrying home to my source. I ask myself: *Is this gold that I have accumulated over the years my gift to God or God's gift to me?* I think it may be a little of both.

God sent Babaji into my life and gave me numerous Divine moments that help me see that I have never been alone and there has been a purpose for my human form. He has shown me again and again that there is a mysterious celestial world within reach and a limitless supply of love and support from that innermost well. I have learned that the main purpose for all of us is to learn to love—ourselves, each other and our real mother, who is the Earth. We are called to recognize that we are all the same and intrinsically connected to each other through the spark of divinity that we all carry.

My gift to Her may be the love and awe and gratitude I feel for Her daily and the trust I have placed in Her over the years as I yielded to Her hands.

Once again, I am reminded of the boy who bought the Christmas ornament for his mother. I feel that I am carrying my treasure home to God, as well as sharing it with others following behind me. This book has been a way to capture and preserve it so the same thing that happened to that young boy many years ago does not happen to me.

It has not always been an easy journey, and it has required an investment and commitment to an inner path that was often treacherous and lonely, and which could not be seen clearly nor easily understood. Yogananda reminds me of the Source of this challenge when He says: *Oh Divine Sculptor, chisel Thou my life to 'Thy design!*[1] I have been certainly been hacked and chiseled by Babaji, and I have participated, even though it was not always enthusiastically. Yes, at my birth, I was poured into the die of an orphan, but God and Babaji have transformed that mold, revealing more and more of my Divine nature and drawing me closer to Him. Has it been worth it? I say emphatically: "YES!"

The process of writing this book has resulted in my loving my parents more than I ever had before. I have been able to understand them and see them as human beings trying to do their best during very difficult times and with no guidance. I have been able to truly forgive them and myself for the lack of understanding. I wish I knew then what I know now, but I realize it is never too late to mend bridges and learn to love more.

Life has really been a path of fire for me, and I realize that the fire burns away everything that stands between ourselves and God until we become love and light in action. It is an ongoing process of transformation with rich rewards. It is a journey from the head to the heart and to the Self, or glorious center of who we are, from which everything else radiates.

I hope I am facing the next adventure with a sense of awe, curiosity and trepidation, but also with love, gratitude, trust and humility.

When all outer patterns are shown to be deceptive, one can either struggle amidst the destruction, trying to cling onto the ruins, or one can leave behind any outer form or identification, and turn inward where the only true belonging exists.[2]

—From *The Face Before I Was Born,*
by Llewellyn Vaughan-Lee

Notes

[1] Paramahansa Yogananda, *Whispers from Eternity*, p. 29.

[2] Llewellyn Vaughn-Lee, *The Face Before I was Born*, p. 292.

Personal Thoughts

REFERENCES

Altea, Rosemary. n.d. *Azquotes*. Accessed 02 13, 2021. https://azquotes.com/author/23946-Rosemary-Altea.

Buechner, Frederick. 1977. *Telling the Truth: The Gospel as Tragedy, Comedy, and Fairy Tale*. San Francisco: Harper.

Campbell, Joseph. n.d. *The Hero's Journey*.

Cayce, Edgar. n.d. "Search for God, Books 1 and 2."

Chase, Tamlorn. n.d. *Odyssey Online, Antioch University*. Accessed 02 13, 2021. https://odyssey.antiochsb.edu/literary/joseph-campbell-the-heros-journey/.

Chopra, Deepak. n.d. *Goodreads*. Accessed 02 13, 2021. www.goodreads.com/quotes/93256.

Devotees, Edited by group of Babaji's. 1999. "Babaji Mahavatar—the descent of Eternity into time." Vrijenbergweg: Haidakhandi Samaj Foundation.

Estes, Clarissa Pinkola. 1992. *Women who run with the wolves*. New York: Random House , Inc.

Gide, Andre. n.d. *Goodreads*. Accessed 02 13, 2021. www.goodreads.com/quotes/192564.

Goodman, Dr Shdema. 1986. *Babaji—Meeting with Truth.* Author.

Johnson, Robert. 1998. *Balancing Heaven and Earth.* New York, NY: Harper Collins.
—1991. "Owning Your Own Shadow." New York, NY: Harper Collins.

Jung, C.G. 1969. *CW Volume 8—The Structure and Dynamics of the Psyche. 2nd edition.* Princeton, NJ: Princeton University Press.
—1961. *Memories, Dreams and Reflections-translated by Richard and Clara Winston, edited by Aniela Jaffe.* Toronto, Canada: Random House Inc., Pantheon Books.

Kreinheder, Albert. 2009. *Body and Soul.* Toronto, Canada: Inner City Books.

Mandell, Arnold. 1982. *Dreambody—The Body's Role In Revealing the Self.* Santa Monica, CA: SIGO press.

Miyamoto, Shigeru. n.d. *Goodreads*. Accessed 02 13, 2021. www.goodreads.com/quotes/360610.

Pert, Candace. n.d. *Azquotes*. Accessed 02 14, 2020. https://azquotes.com/author/24367-Candace_Pert.

Reichel, Gertrude, editor. 1986. *Babaji—The Unfathomable.* Haidakhandi Samaj.

Reis, Patricia. 1997. *Daughters of Saturn*. New York, NY: The Continuum Publishing Co.

Samaj, Haidakhandi. 1983. *The Teachings of Babaji*. District Nainital, India: Haidakhandi Samaj.

Sawin, Leslie, Lionel Corbett, and MIchael Carbine, editors. 2014. *Jung and Aging*. New Orleans, LA: Spring Journal Inc.

Shastriji. 1985. *Haidiyakhandi Sapta Sati*. Nainital, India: Haidakhandi Samaj.

Shyam, Radhe. 1990. *I am Harmony—A book about Babaji*. Crestone. CO: American Haidakhan Samaj.

Tick, Edward. 2005. *War and the Soul*. Wheaton, IL: Quest Books.

Toynbee, Arnold Dr. n.d. *Reddit*. Accessed 02 13, 2021. reddit.com/r/aznidentity/comments/kmslyu/ this_quote_sums_up_western_civilization_barbarism.

Tweedie, Irina. 1989. *Daughter of Fire*. Nevada City, CA: Blue Dolphin Publishing.

Vaughan-Lee, Llewellyn. 1998. *The Face Before I was Born*. Inverness, CA: The Golden Sufi Center.

Verlag, Reichel G. 1990. *Babaji—Message from the Himalayas*. West Germany: Haidakhandi Samaj.

Woodman, Marion and Jill Mellick. 2000. *Coming Home to Myself*. Boston, MA: Conari Press.

Woodman, Marion. 1993. *Conscious Femininity*. Toronto, ON Canada: Inner City Books.
—n.d. "Marion Woodman Foundation Body Soul Rhythm's® Leadership Training Workshops." London, ON Canada.
—1985. *The Pregnant Virgin—A Process of Psychological Transformation*. Toronto, Canada: Inner City Books.
—1990. *The Ravaged Bridegroom—Masculinity in Women*. Toronto, Canada: Inner City Books.

Yogananda, Paramahansa. 1994. *Autobiography of a Yogi*. Los Angeles, CA: Self Realization Fellowship.
—1992. *Whispers from Eternity*. Los Angeles, CA: Self-Realization Fellowship.

LINKS TO LEARN MORE

Haidakhandi Universal Ashram in USA (Babajiashram.org)
American Haidakhan Samaj (BabajiSamaj.us)
Haidakhan Ashram in India (HaidakhandiSamaj.in)
Haidakhan Indian Samaj (HaidakhandiSamaj.in)
Marion Woodman Foundation (MWoodmanFoundation.org)
Christina Thomas-Fraser (ctfraser22@gmail.com)
Patricia Reis (PatriciaReis.net)
International Babaji Ashrams and Centers
(HaidakhandiSamaj.in)

ACKNOWLEDGMENTS

There are so many people I would like to thank who made this book possible:

To my childhood friends, Shena McDonald nee Fulton, Rosemary Smith nee Titmuss and Sue Hunt nee Wyper, for recognizing something in me so many years ago (when we were all so young) and for providing a lifelong friendship.

To Mrs. Titmuss for being my second mum when I needed one so desperately.

To my Nan, who spoke so honestly to me about a spirit world and opened my eyes from an early age.

To my parents, Amy and Ray Winters, for giving me the gift of life and without whom I could never have made this journey.

To Verna Woods, who was another mother and confidant when I was so lost in Canada. She was the only person I could talk to about my spiritual beliefs and experiences.

Huge thanks to Christina Thomas -Fraser, my spiritual mother who created the love and space for Babaji to enter my life, for never giving up on me.

To my UK family and my US family, who love me and are always there for me. I have never shared my story with them until now.

To Carl Jung, for birthing a new psychology and providing a framework for the understanding of psychology and spirituality. His work continues to evolve.

I have enormous gratitude for the teachers and guides who supported me directly or through their books: Marion Woodman, Robert Johnson, members of the Memphis Jung Seminar, my spiritual family at the Haidakhan Universal Ashram, Irina Tweedie, Llewellyn Vaughn Lee, Ed Tick and too many others to name.

To Ramloti (Deborah Wood), for her supreme dedication to Babaji and the Divine Mother, and for holding the ashram space over the last 30 years so thousands of us could be inspired and guided and our lives enriched in inconceivable ways.

To Jonathan and Premanand for their dedication, loyalty and hard work for 30 years, helping to maintain Divine Mother's and Babaji's home at the foot of the Sangre de Cristo Mountains.

To Patricia Reis, who was instrumental in getting me to India and helping me to understand my destiny.

To my Florida Babaji team, Sharda and Jeffrey Solomon and Sal and Sarena Morello, and their dedication to Babaji and the Sacred Fire.

To my adopted family in Colorado, Sabina and AJ and Shreyash and Azelia, who provide so much love and inspiration.

To the children in my life who are now grown: Nicole, Shelly Michael and Sandra, Lexie and Erin, Natalie, Natasha, Zienna, Hannah and Isaac. Thank you for your youthful exuberance and for letting me into your hearts.

To my editor, Nirmala Nataraj, my coach, Michelle Gano, my formatter, Debbie Lum and the community at SPS, who were my chief cheerleaders and believed I could do this.

To Meg Wilbur for being the midwife who helped birth this book.

To the Marion Woodman community, who provided a safe space for me to be me and come home to my body.

To my friends, Colleen Dupont and Carol Shain, who provided support over the phone and in person, over coffee, on an ongoing basis.

To Susana McCall, who read early drafts and kept me going with bimonthly phone calls and unending validation and support.

To Tammie Holloway, who was always a calming presence and made sure my body and energy were up to the task with her intuitive energy work and massage.

To all my clients who are so open to taking this inner path. I learn so much from you, and I continue to be inspired.

Huge thanks to JD at jdmarston.photoshelter.com for providing the beautiful picture of Divine Mother that appears on the cover.

Grateful thanks to Andrea Wells at wildsoulconservation.com for being our BodySoul ® photographer and providing the picture of me with Marion Woodman, which appears on the cover.

Heartfelt thanks to the international Babaji community for the love and devotion they carry for the radiance of Babaji— offering truth, simplicity and love to Mother Earth and all beings.

Deep gratitude for the beauty and wisdom I found in *Babaji Mahavatar: The Descent of Eternity into Time*, published by the Babaji Community in Holland, and the book *Meeting with Truth*, by Shdema Goodman.

Many thanks to Marie-Gabriele Wosen and the publisher Reichel Verlag for permission to quote from *Babaji: Message from the Himalayas*.

Grateful thanks to the Indian Samaj and American Haidakhan Samaj for permission to quote from *The Teachings of Babaji and Babaji the Unfathomable*.

Sincere gratitude and appreciation to the American Haidakhan Samaj for permission to quote from *I Am Harmony*, by Radhe Shyam/Charles Swan and Haidakhan Sapti Sati , by Vishnu Datt Shastriji, as well as the beautiful poetry that pours from these pages.

To my son Tom Jr (Tommy) for loving me and accepting me as your 'second mom' and to Heather for giving so much love to both of us. I love you both so much.

To my late husband, Tom: Thanks for staying by my side through thick and thin and teaching me that love becomes stronger and more durable through the toughest times.

And last but not least, to Babaji, Muniraji and the Divine Mother, who are always with me and who have changed me and my life in a miraculous manner.

ABOUT THE AUTHOR

Elaine Heroux has a master's degree in Psychology from the University of Tennessee. She is a qualified Licensed Clinical Social Worker (LCSW) and has a private practice. She studied for a year at the Authentic Movement Institute in San Francisco and then trained under Jungian analyst Marion Woodman in her BodySoul® Leadership Training program for four years. Elaine has been a follower of Haidakhan Babaji for 30 years and currently lives in Florida. For more information, go to www.innerway.com.

SELF-PUBLISHING SCHOOL

NOW IT'S YOUR TURN

Discover the EXACT 3-step blueprint you need to become a bestselling author in as little as 3 months.

Self-Publishing School helped me, and now I want them to help you with this FREE resource to begin outlining your book!

Even if you're busy, bad at writing, or don't know where to start, you CAN write a bestseller and build your best life.

With tools and experience across a variety of niches and professions,

Self-Publishing School is the only resource you need to take your book to the finish line!

DON'T WAIT

Say "YES" to becoming a bestseller:
https://self-publishingschool.com/friend/

Follow the steps on the page to get a FREE resource to get started on your book and unlock a discount to get started with Self-Publishing School

WILL YOU HELP?

Thank you for reading my book!

I really appreciate all your feedback and I love hearing
what you have to say.
I welcome your input to make the next version of this
book and my future books better.

Please leave an honest review on Amazon letting me
know what you think of this.
Thank you so much!

Elaine Heroux

Made in United States
North Haven, CT
22 December 2022

29980610R00147